Knowing His Promises

God's direction for my life

Knowing His Promises
God's Direction for My Life

ISBN 0-9679816-0-3
Copyright © 2000 by Ron Warren

Abiding Life Publisher
P.O. Box 62032
Ft. Myers, FL 33906

Art Direction and Graphic Design by:
Creation Studios, Inc.
www.creationstudios.net

1st. Printing, November 2000
2nd Printing January 2002

Unless otherwise indicated, all scripture quotations are
taken from the King James Version.

Forward

Knowing His Promises, is to challenge you to abide in the Word, and to seek the face of our great God and Lord and Savior, Jesus Christ.

On the cover of this book (Knowing His Promises) you will see a compass, representing God's direction for your life with God's exciting promises. God has a plan and purpose for your life, and it is found in his promises.

You will see the lighthouse on the cover, it represents the Word of God which brings light to our life in a dark and unclear world.

The sexton represents, being able to focus our lives according to the promises of God. A focused Christian will reach their potential in Christ.

Abiding Life Publisher

Part 1

PART I • SOUND MIND

Guidance...................................7-16

Comfort...................................17-28

Forgiveness.............................29-34

Fear Not.................................35-44

Renewed Mind.........................45-56

Encouragement........................57-62

Part 2

PART II • OH MY SOUL

Victory...................................63-70

Courage.................................71-80

Faith.....................................81-90

Healing.................................91-100

Strength...............................101-110

Witnessing............................111-118

Part 3

PART III • RENEW MY SPIRIT

Salvation..............................119-130

Relationships........................131-138

Praise..................................139-144

Trust....................................145-156

Love of God...........................157-164

Prayer..................................165-178

Prayer Journal.......................179-183

Answers to Questions..................187

PART 1 • SOUND MIND

Guidance

GENESIS 12:1

Now the Lord had said unto Abram, Get thee out of thy country, and from thy kindred, and from thy father's house, unto a land that I will shew thee:

EXODUS 13:21

And the Lord went before them by day in a pillar of a cloud, to lead them the way; and by night in a pillar of fire, to give them light; to go by day and night:

EXODUS 15:13

Thou in thy mercy hast led forth the people which thou hast redeemed: thou hast guided them in thy strength unto thy holy habitation.

EXODUS 33:13-15

Now therefore, I pray thee, if I have found grace in thy sight, shew me now thy way, that I may know thee, that I may find grace in thy sight: and consider that this nation is thy people.

And he said, My presence shall go with thee, and I will give thee rest.

And he said unto him, If thy presence go not with me, carry us not up hence.

2 SAMUEL 22:29

For thou art my lamp, O Lord: and the Lord will lighten my darkness.

GUIDANCE

Knowing His Promises

NUMBERS 10:33

And they departed from the mount of the Lord three days' journey: and the ark of the covenant of the Lord went before them in the three days' journey, to search out a resting place for them.

DEUTERONOMY 32:10,12

He found him in a desert land, and in the waste howling wilderness; he led him about, he instructed him, he kept him as the apple of his eye.

So the Lord alone did lead him, and there was no strange God with him.

2 CHRONICLES 32:22

Thus the Lord saved Hezekiah and the inhabitants of Jerusalem from the hand of Sennacherib the king of Assyria, and from the hand of all other, and guided them on every side.

NEHEMIAH 9:19-20

Yet thou in thy manifold mercies forsookest them not in the wilderness: the pillar of the cloud departed not from them by day, to lead them in the way; neither the pillar of fire by night, to shew them light, and the way wherein they should go.

Thou gavest also thy good spirit to instruct them, and withheldest not thy manna from their mouth, and gavest them water for their thirst.

PSALMS 5:8

Lead me, O Lord, in thy righteousness because of mine enemies; make thy way straight before my face.

Part 1 • Sound Mind • *Guidance*

PSALMS 23:2,3

> He maketh me to lie down in green pastures: he leadeth me beside the still waters.
>
> He restoreth my soul: he leadeth me in the paths of righteousness for his name's sake.

PSALMS 25:5

> Lead me in thy truth, and teach me: for thou art the God of my salvation; on thee do I wait all the day.

PSALMS 25:9

> The meek will he guide in judgment: and the meek will he teach his way.

PSALMS 27:11

> Teach me thy way, O Lord, and lead me in a plain path, because of mine enemies.

PSALMS 31:3

> For thou art my rock and my fortress; therefore for thy name's sake lead me, and guide me.

PSALMS 32:8

> I will instruct thee and teach thee in the way which thou shalt go: I will guide thee with mine eye.

PSALMS 48:14

> For this God is our God for ever and ever: he will be our guide even unto death.

PSALMS 61:2

> From the end of the earth will I cry unto thee, when my heart is overwhelmed: lead me to the rock that is higher than I.

GUIDANCE

Knowing His Promises

PSALMS 73:24

> Thou shalt guide me with thy counsel, and afterward receive me to glory.

PSALMS 78:52

> But made his own people to go forth like sheep, and guided them in the wilderness like a flock.

PSALMS 80:1

> Give ear, O Shepherd of Israel, thou that leadest Joseph like a flock; thou that dwellest between the cherubims, shine forth.

PSALMS 107:7

> And he led them forth by the right way, that they might go to a city of habitation.

PSALMS 119:105

> Thy word is a lamp unto my feet, and a light unto my path.

PSALMS 139:9-10,24

> If I take the wings of the morning, and dwell in the uttermost parts of the sea;
>
> Even there shall thy hand lead me, and thy right hand shall hold me.
>
> And see if there be any wicked way in me, and lead me in the way everlasting.

PROVERBS 3:5-6

> Trust in the Lord with all thine heart; and lean not unto thine own understanding.
>
> In all thy ways acknowledge him, and he shall direct thy paths.

Guidance

PROVERBS 8:20

> I lead in the way of righteousness, in the midst of the paths of judgment:

ISAIAH 40:11

> He shall feed his flock like a shepherd: he shall gather the lambs with his arm, and carry them in his bosom, and shall gently lead those that are with young.

ISAIAH 42:16

> And I will bring the blind by a way that they knew not; I will lead them in paths that they have not known: I will make darkness light before them, and crooked things straight. These things will I do unto them, and not forsake them.

ISAIAH 48:17

> Thus saith the Lord, thy Redeemer, the Holy One of Israel; I am the Lord thy God which teacheth thee to profit, which leadeth thee by the way that thou shouldest go.

ISAIAH 57:18

> I have seen his ways, and will heal him: I will lead him also, and restore comforts unto him and to his mourners.

ISAIAH 58:11

> And the Lord shall guide thee continually, and satisfy thy soul in drought, and make fat thy bones: and thou shalt be like a watered garden, and like a spring of water, whose waters fail not.

JEREMIAH 3:4

> Wilt thou not from this time cry unto me, My father, thou art the guide of my youth?

GUIDANCE

Knowing His Promises

LUKE 1:79

To give light to them that sit in darkness and in the shadow of death, to guide our feet into the way of peace.

JOHN 10:3-4

To him the porter openeth; and the sheep hear his voice: and he calleth his own sheep by name, and leadeth them out.

And when he putteth forth his own sheep, he goeth before them, and the sheep follow him: for they know his voice.

JAMES 1:5-8

If any of you lack wisdom, let him ask of God, that giveth to all men liberally, and upbraideth not; and it shall be given him.

But let him ask in faith, nothing wavering. For he that wavereth is like a wave of the sea driven with the wind and tossed.

For let not that man think that he shall receive any thing of the Lord.

A double minded man is unstable in all his ways.

1 CORINTHIANS 1:30

But of him are ye in Christ Jesus, who of God is made unto us wisdom, and righteousness, and sanctification, and redemption:

JOSHUA 1:8

This book of the law shall not depart out of thy mouth; but thou shalt meditate therein day and night, that thou mayest observe to do according to all that is written therein: for then thou shalt make thy way prosperous, and then thou shalt have good success.

1 CORINTHIANS 2:9-10

But as it is written, Eye hath not seen, nor ear heard, neither have entered into the heart of man, the things which God hath prepared for them that love him.

But God hath revealed them unto us by his Spirit: for the Spirit searcheth all things, yea, the deep things of God.

DEUTERONOMY 28:1-2

And it shall come to pass, if thou shalt hearken diligently unto the voice of the Lord thy God, to observe and to do all his commandments which I command thee this day, that the Lord thy God will set thee on high above all nations of the earth:

And all these blessings shall come on thee, and overtake thee, if thou shalt hearken unto the voice of the Lord thy God.

ISAIAH 55:2-3

Wherefore do ye spend money for that which is not bread? and your labor for that which satisfieth not? hearken diligently unto me, and eat ye that which is good, and let your soul delight itself in fatness.

Incline your ear, and come unto me: hear, and your soul shall live; and I will make an everlasting covenant with you, even the sure mercies of David.

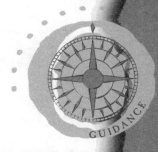

Part I

Comfort

PSALMS 69:29-30

> But I am poor and sorrowful: let thy salvation, O God, set me up on high.

> I will praise the name of God with a song, and will magnify him with thanksgiving.

JOHN 14:16

> And I will pray the Father, and he shall give you another Comforter, that he may abide with you for ever;

PSALMS 42:11

> Why art thou cast down, O my soul? and why art thou disquieted within me? hope thou in God: for I shall yet praise him, who is the health of my countenance, and my God.

HEBREWS 4:16

> Let us therefore come boldly unto the throne of grace, that we may obtain mercy, and find grace to help in time of need.

PSALMS 119:50

> This is my comfort in my affliction: for thy word hath quickened me.

JEREMIAH 31:25

> For I have satiated the weary soul, and I have replenished every sorrowful soul.

15

Knowing His Promises

2 Corinthians 1:3-4

Blessed be God, even the Father of our Lord Jesus Christ, the Father of mercies, and the God of all comfort;

Who comforteth us in all our tribulation, that we may be able to comfort them which are in any trouble, by the comfort wherewith we ourselves are comforted of God.

Isaiah 50:10

Who is among you that feareth the Lord, that obeyeth the voice of his servant, that walketh in darkness, and hath no light? let him trust in the name of the Lord, and stay upon his God.

Psalms 18:4-6

The sorrows of death compassed me, and the floods of ungodly men made me afraid.

The sorrows of hell compassed me about: the snares of death prevented me.

In my distress I called upon the Lord, and cried unto my God: he heard my voice out of his temple, and my cry came before him, even into his ears.

Psalms 119:28

My soul melteth for heaviness: strengthen thou me according unto thy word.

Psalms 63:1

O God, thou art my God; early will I seek thee: my soul thirsteth for thee, my flesh longeth for thee in a dry and thirsty land, where no water is;

PSALMS 30:5

For his anger endureth but a moment; in his favor is life: weeping may endure for a night, but joy cometh in the morning.

EZRA 9:5

And at the evening sacrifice I arose up from my heaviness; and having rent my garment and my mantle, I fell upon my knees, and spread out my hands unto the Lord my God,

PSALMS 42:6-7

O my God, my soul is cast down within me: therefore will I remember thee from the land of Jordan, and of the Hermonites, from the hill Mizar.

Deep calleth unto deep at the noise of thy waterspouts: all thy waves and thy billows are gone over me.

PSALMS 31:19-21

Oh how great is thy goodness, which thou hast laid up for them that fear thee; which thou hast wrought for them that trust in thee before the sons of men!

Thou shalt hide them in the secret of thy presence from the pride of man: thou shalt keep them secretly in a pavilion from the strife of tongues.

Blessed be the Lord: for he hath shewed me his marvellous kindness in a strong city.

MATTHEW 10:30

But the very hairs of your head are all numbered.

PROVERBS 12:25

Heaviness in the heart of man maketh it stoop: but a good word maketh it glad.

Knowing His Promises

JOHN 14:1

Let not your heart be troubled: ye believe in God, believe also in me.

PSALMS 62:8

Trust in him at all times; ye people, pour out your heart before him: God is a refuge for us. Selah.

PSALMS 34:5

They looked unto him, and were lightened: and their faces were not ashamed.

ISAIAH 66:13-14

As one whom his mother comforteth, so will I comfort you; and ye shall be comforted in Jerusalem.

And when ye see this, your heart shall rejoice, and your bones shall flourish like an herb: and the hand of the Lord shall be known toward his servants, and his indignation toward his enemies.

PSALMS 32:10-11

Many sorrows shall be to the wicked: but he that trusteth in the Lord, mercy shall compass him about.

Be glad in the Lord, and rejoice, ye righteous: and shout for joy, all ye that are upright in heart.

DEUTERONOMY 33:27

The eternal God is thy refuge, and underneath are the everlasting arms: and he shall thrust out the enemy from before thee; and shall say, Destroy them.

PROVERBS 18:14

The spirit of a man will sustain his infirmity; but a wounded spirit who can bear?

PSALMS 69:32-34

The humble shall see this, and be glad: and your heart shall live that seek God.

For the Lord heareth the poor, and despiseth not his prisoners.

Let the heaven and earth praise him, the seas, and every thing that moveth therein.

PSALMS 34:4,7

I sought the Lord, and he heard me, and delivered me from all my fears.

The angel of the Lord encampeth round about them that fear him, and delivereth them.

PSALMS 63:3-7

Because thy loving kindness is better than life, my lips shall praise thee.

Thus will I bless thee while I live: I will lift up my hands in thy name.

My soul shall be satisfied as with marrow and fatness; and my mouth shall praise thee with joyful lips:

When I remember thee upon my bed, and meditate on thee in the night watches.

Because thou hast been my help, therefore in the shadow of thy wings will I rejoice.

ISAIAH 61:3

To appoint unto them that mourn in Zion, to give unto them beauty for ashes, the oil of joy for mourning, the garment of praise for the spirit of heaviness; that they might be called trees of righteousness, the planting of the Lord, that he might be glorified.

19

Knowing His Promises

PSALMS 56:8-10

Thou tellest my wanderings: put thou my tears into thy
bottle: are they not in thy book?
When I cry unto thee, then shall mine enemies turn back:
this I know; for God is for me.
In God will I praise his word: in the Lord will I praise
his word.

PSALMS 31:7

I will be glad and rejoice in thy mercy: for thou hast con-
sidered my trouble; thou hast known my soul in adversi-
ties;

PSALMS 94:19

In the multitude of my thoughts within me thy comforts
delight my soul.

ISAIAH 25:4

For thou hast been a strength to the poor, a strength to
the needy in his distress, a refuge from the storm, a shadow from the heat, when the blast of the terrible ones is as
a storm against the wall.

EXODUS 14:13-14

And Moses said unto the people, Fear ye not, stand still,
and see the salvation of the Lord, which he will shew to
you to day: for the Egyptians whom ye have seen to day,
ye shall see them again no more for ever.

The Lord shall fight for you, and ye shall hold your
peace.

PSALMS 69:20

Reproach hath broken my heart; and I am full of heaviness: and I looked for some to take pity, but there was
none; and for comforters, but I found none.

PSALMS 34:6

This poor man cried, and the Lord heard him, and saved him out of all his troubles.

PSALMS 41:3

The Lord will strengthen him upon the bed of languishing: thou wilt make all his bed in his sickness.

LUKE 7:13

And when the Lord saw her, he had compassion on her, and said unto her, Weep not.

PSALMS 142:1-3

I cried unto the Lord with my voice; with my voice unto the Lord did I make my supplication.

I poured out my complaint before him; I shewed before him my trouble.

When my spirit was overwhelmed within me, then thou knewest my path. In the way wherein I walked have they privily laid a snare for me.

PSALMS 107:13-14

Then they cried unto the Lord in their trouble, and he saved them out of their distresses.

He brought them out of darkness and the shadow of death, and brake their bands in sunder.

PROVERBS 14:10

The heart knoweth his own bitterness; and a stranger doth not intermeddle with his joy.

2 SAMUEL 22:28

And the afflicted people thou wilt save: but thine eyes are upon the haughty, that thou mayest bring them down.

Knowing His Promises

PSALMS 69:29-30

But I am poor and sorrowful: let thy salvation, O God, set me up on high.
I will praise the name of God with a song, and will magnify him with thanksgiving.

2 CORINTHIANS 12:9

And he said unto me, My grace is sufficient for thee: for my strength is made perfect in weakness. Most gladly therefore will I rather glory in my infirmities, that the power of Christ may rest upon me.

2 CORINTHIANS 6:2

(For he saith, I have heard thee in a time accepted, and in the day of salvation have I succoured thee: behold, now is the accepted time; behold, now is the day of salvation.)

HEBREWS 13:6

So that we may boldly say, The Lord is my helper, and I will not fear what man shall do unto me.

PSALMS 34:8

O taste and see that the Lord is good: blessed is the man that trusteth in him.

2 CORINTHIANS 1:8-9

For we would not, brethren, have you ignorant of our trouble which came to us in Asia, that we were pressed out of measure, above strength, insomuch that we despaired even of life:

But we had the sentence of death in ourselves, that we should not trust in ourselves, but in God which raiseth the dead:

PSALMS 141:8

> But mine eyes are unto thee, O God the Lord: in thee is my trust; leave not my soul destitute.

MATTHEW 14:27

> But straightway Jesus spake unto them, saying, Be of good cheer; it is I; be not afraid.

PSALMS 138:3

> In the day when I cried thou answeredst me, and strengthenedst me with strength in my soul.

EXODUS 3:7-8

> And the Lord said, I have surely seen the affliction of my people which are in Egypt, and have heard their cry by reason of their taskmasters; for I know their sorrows;
>
> And I am come down to deliver them out of the hand of the Egyptians, and to bring them up out of that land unto a good land and a large, unto a land flowing with milk and honey; unto the place of the Canaanites, and the Hittites, and the Amorites, and the Perizzites, and the Hivites, and the Jebusites.

PSALMS 18:32

> It is God that girdeth me with strength, and maketh my way perfect.

MATTHEW 5:4

> Blessed are they that mourn: for they shall be comforted.

NAHUM 1:7

> The Lord is good, a strong hold in the day of trouble; and he knoweth them that trust in him

Knowing His Promises

PSALMS 145:14-19

The Lord upholdeth all that fall, and raiseth up all those that be bowed down.

The eyes of all wait upon thee; and thou givest them their meat in due season.

Thou openest thine hand, and satisfiest the desire of every living thing.

The Lord is righteous in all his ways, and holy in all his works.

The Lord is nigh unto all them that call upon him, to all that call upon him in truth.

He will fulfill the desire of them that fear him: he also will hear their cry, and will save them.

PSALMS 107:6-9

Then they cried unto the Lord in their trouble, and he delivered them out of their distresses.

And he led them forth by the right way, that they might go to a city of habitation.

Oh that men would praise the Lord for his goodness, and for his wonderful works to the children of men!

For he satisfieth the longing soul, and filleth the hungry soul with goodness.

2 CORINTHIANS 4:13-14

We having the same spirit of faith, according as it is written, I believed, and therefore have I spoken; we also believe, and therefore speak;

Knowing that he which raised up the Lord Jesus shall raise up us also by Jesus, and shall present us with you.

PSALMS 9:9-11

> The Lord also will be a refuge for the oppressed, a refuge in times of trouble.
>
> And they that know thy name will put their trust in thee: for thou, Lord, hast not forsaken them that seek thee.
>
> Sing praises to the Lord, which dwelleth in Zion: declare among the people his doings.

PSALMS 119:92-93

> Unless thy law had been my delights, I should then have perished in mine affliction.
>
> I will never forget thy precepts: for with them thou hast quickened me.

ISAIAH 41:13

> For I the Lord thy God will hold thy right hand, saying unto thee, Fear not; I will help thee.

PSALMS 27:5-6

> For in the time of trouble he shall hide me in his pavilion: in the secret of his tabernacle shall he hide me; he shall set me up upon a rock.
>
> And now shall mine head be lifted up above mine enemies round about me: therefore will I offer in his tabernacle sacrifices of joy; I will sing, yea, I will sing praises unto the Lord.

ISAIAH 40:29

> He giveth power to the faint; and to them that have no might he increaseth strength.

PSALMS 31:16

> Make thy face to shine upon thy servant: save me for thy mercies' sake.

Knowing His Promises

ISAIAH 54:11

O thou afflicted, tossed with tempest, and not comforted, behold, I will lay thy stones with fair colors, and lay thy foundations with sapphires.

JEREMIAH 31:13-14

Then shall the virgin rejoice in the dance, both young men and old together: for I will turn their mourning into joy, and will comfort them, and make them rejoice from their sorrow.

And I will satiate the soul of the priests with fatness, and my people shall be satisfied with my goodness, saith the Lord.

PSALMS 107:19-20

Then they cry unto the Lord in their trouble, and he saveth them out of their distresses.

He sent his word, and healed them, and delivered them from their destructions.

PSALMS 31:9-10

Have mercy upon me, O Lord, for I am in trouble: mine eye is consumed with grief, yea, my soul and my belly.

For my life is spent with grief, and my years with sighing: my strength faileth because of mine iniquity, and my bones are consumed.

PSALMS 55:22

Cast thy burden upon the Lord, and he shall sustain thee: he shall never suffer the righteous to be moved.

2 THESSALONIANS 2:16-17

Now our Lord Jesus Christ himself, and God, even our Father, which hath loved us, and hath given us everlasting consolation and good hope through grace,

Comfort your hearts, and stablish you in every good word and work.

ISAIAH 40:31

But they that wait upon the Lord shall renew their strength; they shall mount up with wings as eagles; they shall run, and not be weary; and they shall walk, and not faint.

PSALMS 32:3-5

When I kept silence, my bones waxed old through my roaring all the day long.

For day and night thy hand was heavy upon me: my moisture is turned into the drought of summer. Selah.

I acknowledge my sin unto thee, and mine iniquity have I not hid. I said, I will confess my transgressions unto the Lord; and thou forgavest the iniquity of my sin. Selah.

PSALMS 69:1-3

Save me, O God; for the waters are come in unto my soul.

I sink in deep mire, where there is no standing: I am come into deep waters, where the floods overflow me.

I am weary of my crying: my throat is dried: mine eyes fail while I wait for my God.

Knowing His Promises

PSALMS 119:143

Trouble and anguish have taken hold on me: yet thy commandments are my delights.

2 SAMUEL 22:29

For thou art my lamp, O Lord: and the Lord will lighten my darkness.

JOHN 14:27

Peace I leave with you, my peace I give unto you: not as the world giveth, give I unto you. Let not your heart be troubled, neither let it be afraid.

PSALMS 143:3-4

For the enemy hath persecuted my soul; he hath smitten my life down to the ground; he hath made me to dwell in darkness, as those that have been long dead.

Therefore is my spirit overwhelmed within me; my heart within me is desolate.

PSALMS 31:24

Be of good courage, and he shall strengthen your heart, all ye that hope in the Lord.

Part I

Forgiveness

PSALMS 99:8

Thou answeredst them, O Lord our God: thou wast a
God that forgavest them, though thou tookest vengeance
of their inventions.

COLOSSIANS 2:13

And you, being dead in your sins and the uncircumcision
of your flesh, hath he quickened together with him, having forgiven you all trespasses;

ISAIAH 1:18

Come now, and let us reason together, saith the Lord:
though your sins be as scarlet, they shall be as white as
snow; though they be red like crimson, they shall be as
wool.

EPHESIANS 4:32

And be ye kind one to another, tenderhearted, forgiving
one another, even as God for Christ's sake hath forgiven
you.

ROMANS 4:7-8

Saying, Blessed are they whose iniquities are forgiven,
and whose sins are covered.

Blessed is the man to whom the Lord will not impute
sin.

PSALMS 103:12

As far as the east is from the west, so far hath he
removed our transgressions from us.

Knowing His Promises

LUKE 17:3

Take heed to yourselves: If thy brother trespass against thee, rebuke him; and if he repent, forgive him.

1 JOHN 1:7

But if we walk in the light, as he is in the light, we have fellowship one with another, and the blood of Jesus Christ his Son cleanseth us from all sin.

MATTHEW 9:6

But that ye may know that the Son of man hath power on earth to forgive sins, (then saith he to the sick of the palsy,) Arise, take up thy bed, and go unto thine house.

MATTHEW 6:14-15

For if ye forgive men their trespasses, your heavenly Father will also forgive you:

But if ye forgive not men their trespasses, neither will your Father forgive your trespasses.

PSALMS 85:2

Thou hast forgiven the iniquity of thy people, thou hast covered all their sin. Selah.

PSALMS 130:4

But there is forgiveness with thee, that thou mayest be feared.

PSALMS 32:1

Blessed is he whose transgression is forgiven, whose sin is covered.

MATTHEW 5:39

> But I say unto you, That ye resist not evil: but whosoever shall smite thee on thy right cheek, turn to him the other also.

PROVERBS 19:11

> The discretion of a man deferreth his anger; and it is his glory to pass over a transgression.

PROVERBS 24:29

> Say not, I will do so to him as he hath done to me: I will render to the man according to his work.

JOHN 8:11

> She said, No man, Lord. And Jesus said unto her, Neither do I condemn thee: go, and sin no more.

HEBREWS 10:17-18

> And their sins and iniquities will I remember no more.
>
> Now where remission of these is, there is no more offering for sin.

MARK 11:25-26

> And when ye stand praying, forgive, if ye have ought against any: that your Father also which is in heaven may forgive you your trespasses.
>
> But if ye do not forgive, neither will your Father which is in heaven forgive your trespasses.

ACTS 26:18

> To open their eyes, and to turn them from darkness to light, and from the power of Satan unto God, that they may receive forgiveness of sins, and inheritance among them which are sanctified by faith that is in me.

Knowing His Promises

HEBREWS 9:22

And almost all things are by the law purged with blood; and without shedding of blood is no remission.

MATTHEW 26:28

For this is my blood of the new testament, which is shed for many for the remission of sins.

MATTHEW 18:35

So likewise shall my heavenly Father do also unto you, if ye from your hearts forgive not every one his brother their trespasses.

MATTHEW 5:7

Blessed are the merciful: for they shall obtain mercy.

ACTS 13:38

Be it known unto you therefore, men and brethren, that through this man is preached unto you the forgiveness of sins:

MATTHEW 6:12

And forgive us our debts, as we forgive our debtors.

1 JOHN 1:9

If we confess our sins, he is faithful and just to forgive us our sins, and to cleanse us from all unrighteousness.

EPHESIANS 1:7

In whom we have redemption through his blood, the forgiveness of sins, according to the riches of his grace;

PROVERBS 24:17

Rejoice not when thine enemy falleth, and let not thine heart be glad when he stumbleth:

HEBREWS 8:12

> For I will be merciful to their unrighteousness, and their sins and their iniquities will I remember no more.

COLOSSIANS 3:13

> Forbearing one another, and forgiving one another, if any man have a quarrel against any: even as Christ forgave you, so also do ye.

MATTHEW 5:43-44

> Ye have heard that it hath been said, Thou shalt love thy neighbor, and hate thine enemy.
>
> But I say unto you, Love your enemies, bless them that curse you, do good to them that hate you, and pray for them which despitefully use you, and persecute you;

PART 1 • SOUND MIND

Fear Not

2 KINGS 1:15

And the angel of the Lord said unto Elijah, Go down with him: be not afraid of him. And he arose, and went down with him unto the king.

1 PETER 3:14

But and if ye suffer for righteousness' sake, happy are ye: and be not afraid of their terror, neither be troubled;

ISAIAH 12:2

Behold, God is my salvation; I will trust, and not be afraid: for the Lord Jehovah is my strength and my song; he also is become my salvation.

ISAIAH 35:4

Say to them that are of a fearful heart, Be strong, fear not: behold, your God will come with vengeance, even God with a recompence; he will come and save you.

ISAIAH 7:4

And say unto him, Take heed, and be quiet; fear not, neither be fainthearted for the two tails of these smoking firebrands, for the fierce anger of Rezin with Syria, and of the son of Remaliah.

JOSHUA 8:1

And the Lord said unto Joshua, Fear not, neither be thou dismayed: take all the people of war with thee, and arise, go up to Ai: see, I have given into thy hand the king of Ai, and his people, and his city, and his land:

Knowing His Promises

DEUTERONOMY 1:17

Ye shall not respect persons in judgment; but ye shall hear the small as well as the great; ye shall not be afraid of the face of man; for the judgment is God's: and the cause that is too hard for you, bring it unto me, and I will hear it.

ZECHARIAH 8:13

And it shall come to pass, that as ye were a curse among the heathen, O house of Judah, and house of Israel; so will I save you, and ye shall be a blessing: fear not, but let your hands be strong.

2 KINGS 6:16

And he answered, Fear not: for they that be with us are more than they that be with them.

PSALMS 3:6

I will not be afraid of ten thousands of people, that have set themselves against me round about.

ISAIAH 40:9

O Zion, that bringest good tidings, get thee up into the high mountain; O Jerusalem, that bringest good tidings, lift up thy voice with strength; lift it up, be not afraid; say unto the cities of Judah, Behold your God!

JOHN 6:20

But he saith unto them, It is I; be not afraid.

MATTHEW 28:10

Then said Jesus unto them, Be not afraid: go tell my brethren that they go into Galilee, and there shall they see me.

Part 1 • Sound Mind • *Fear Not*

JOSHUA 11:6

And the Lord said unto Joshua, Be not afraid because of them: for to morrow about this time will I deliver them up all slain before Israel: thou shalt hough their horses, and burn their chariots with fire.

1 JOHN 4:18

There is no fear in love; but perfect love casteth out fear: because fear hath torment. He that feareth is not made perfect in love.

ISAIAH 54:15

Behold, they shall surely gather together, but not by me: whosoever shall gather together against thee shall fall for thy sake.

MALACHI 3:5

And I will come near to you to judgment; and I will be a swift witness against the sorcerers, and against the adulterers, and against false swearers, and against those that oppress the hireling in his wages, the widow, and the fatherless, and that turn aside the stranger from his right, and fear not me, saith the Lord of hosts.

JOEL 2:21

Fear not, O land; be glad and rejoice: for the Lord will do great things.

PROVERBS 3:24

When thou liest down, thou shalt not be afraid: yea, thou shalt lie down, and thy sleep shall be sweet.

PSALMS 112:8

His heart is established, he shall not be afraid, until he see his desire upon his enemies.

Knowing His Promises

DEUTERONOMY 31:6

Be strong and of a good courage, fear not, nor be afraid of them: for the Lord thy God, he it is that doth go with thee; he will not fail thee, nor forsake thee.

LUKE 1:30

And the angel said unto her, Fear not, Mary: for thou hast found favor with God.

DEUTERONOMY 3:22

Ye shall not fear them: for the Lord your God he shall fight for you.

PSALMS 56:4

In God I will praise his word, in God I have put my trust; I will not fear what flesh can do unto me.

JEREMIAH 23:4

And I will set up shepherds over them which shall feed them: and they shall fear no more, nor be dismayed, neither shall they be lacking, saith the Lord.

PSALMS 27:1

The Lord is my light and my salvation; whom shall I fear? the Lord is the strength of my life; of whom shall I be afraid?

PSALMS 112:7

He shall not be afraid of evil tidings: his heart is fixed, trusting in the Lord.

LUKE 12:32

Fear not, little flock; for it is your Father's good pleasure to give you the kingdom.

Part 1 • Sound Mind • *Fear Not*

PSALMS 91:5

> Thou shalt not be afraid for the terror by night; nor for the arrow that flieth by day;

EXODUS 20:20

> And Moses said unto the people, Fear not: for God is come to prove you, and that his fear may be before your faces, that ye sin not.

JUDGES 6:10

> And I said unto you, I am the Lord your God; fear not the gods of the Amorites, in whose land ye dwell: but ye have not obeyed my voice.

DANIEL 10:12

> Then said he unto me, Fear not, Daniel: for from the first day that thou didst set thine heart to understand, and to chasten thyself before thy God, thy words were heard, and I am come for thy words.

DEUTERONOMY 20:3

> And shall say unto them, Hear, O Israel, ye approach this day unto battle against your enemies: let not your hearts faint, fear not, and do not tremble, neither be ye terrified because of them;

HEBREWS 13:6

> So that we may boldly say, The Lord is my helper, and I will not fear what man shall do unto me.

GENESIS 26:24

> And the Lord appeared unto him the same night, and said, I am the God of Abraham thy father: fear not, for I am with thee, and will bless thee, and multiply thy seed for my servant Abraham's sake.

Knowing His Promises

1 Kings 17:13

And Elijah said unto her, Fear not; go and do as thou hast said: but make me thereof a little cake first, and bring it unto me, and after make for thee and for thy son.

Jeremiah 46:27

But fear not thou, O my servant Jacob, and be not dismayed, O Israel: for, behold, I will save thee from afar off, and thy seed from the land of their captivity; and Jacob shall return, and be in rest and at ease, and none shall make him afraid.

Isaiah 43:5

Fear not: for I am with thee: I will bring thy seed from the east, and gather thee from the west;

Deuteronomy 31:8

And the Lord, he it is that doth go before thee; he will be with thee, he will not fail thee, neither forsake thee: fear not, neither be dismayed.

Isaiah 44:2

Thus saith the Lord that made thee, and formed thee from the womb, which will help thee; Fear not, O Jacob, my servant; and thou, Jesurun, whom I have chosen.

Joshua 10:25

And Joshua said unto them, Fear not, nor be dismayed, be strong and of good courage: for thus shall the Lord do to all your enemies against whom ye fight.

Deuteronomy 7:18

Thou shalt not be afraid of them: but shalt well remember what the Lord thy God did unto Pharaoh, and unto all Egypt;

JOSHUA 1:9

Have not I commanded thee? Be strong and of a good courage; be not afraid, neither be thou dismayed: for the Lord thy God is with thee whithersoever thou goest.

1 CHRONICLES 28:20

And David said to Solomon his son, Be strong and of good courage, and do it: fear not, nor be dismayed: for the Lord God, even my God, will be with thee; he will not fail thee, nor forsake thee, until thou hast finished all the work for the service of the house of the Lord.

MATTHEW 17:7

And Jesus came and touched them, and said, Arise, and be not afraid.

PSALMS 27:3

Though an host should encamp against me, my heart shall not fear: though war should rise against me, in this will I be confident.

EZEKIEL 2:6

And thou, son of man, be not afraid of them, neither be afraid of their words, though briers and thorns be with thee, and thou dost dwell among scorpions: be not afraid of their words, nor be dismayed at their looks, though they be a rebellious house.

PROVERBS 3:25

Be not afraid of sudden fear, neither of the desolation of the wicked, when it cometh.

DEUTERONOMY 20:1

When thou goest out to battle against thine enemies, and seest horses, and chariots, and a people more than thou, be not afraid of them: for the Lord thy God is with thee, which brought thee up out of the land of Egypt.

Knowing His Promises

PSALMS 118:16

The right hand of the Lord is exalted: the right hand of the Lord doeth valiantly.

LUKE 8:50

But when Jesus heard it, he answered him, saying, Fear not: believe only, and she shall be made whole.

GENESIS 35:17

And it came to pass, when she was in hard labor, that the midwife said unto her, Fear not; thou shalt have this son also.

GENESIS 15:1

After these things the word of the Lord came unto Abram in a vision, saying, Fear not, Abram: I am thy shield, and thy exceeding great reward.

CHRONICLES 20:17

Ye shall not need to fight in this battle: set yourselves, stand ye still, and see the salvation of the Lord with you, O Judah and Jerusalem: fear not, nor be dismayed; tomorrow go out against them: for the Lord will be with you.

GENESIS 21:17

And God heard the voice of the lad; and the angel of God called to Hagar out of heaven, and said unto her, What aileth thee, Hagar? fear not; for God hath heard the voice of the lad where he is.

1 SAMUEL 12:20

And Samuel said unto the people, Fear not: ye have done all this wickedness: yet turn not aside from following the Lord, but serve the Lord with all your heart;

ISAIAH 41:14

Fear not, thou worm Jacob, and ye men of Israel; I will help thee, saith the Lord, and thy redeemer, the Holy One of Israel.

ISAIAH 43:1

But now thus saith the Lord that created thee, O Jacob, and he that formed thee, O Israel, Fear not: for I have redeemed thee, I have called thee by thy name; thou art mine.

ACTS 27:24

Saying, Fear not, Paul; thou must be brought before Caesar: and, lo, God hath given thee all them that sail with thee.

JUDGES 6:23

And the Lord said unto him, Peace be unto thee; fear not: thou shalt not die.

ISAIAH 54:4

Fear not; for thou shalt not be ashamed: neither be thou confounded; for thou shalt not be put to shame: for thou shalt forget the shame of thy youth, and shalt not remember the reproach of thy widowhood any more.

ISAIAH 41:13

For I the Lord thy God will hold thy right hand, saying unto thee, Fear not; I will help thee.

PSALMS 56:11

In God have I put my trust: I will not be afraid what man can do unto me.

Knowing His Promises

RUTH 3:11

And now, my daughter, fear not; I will do to thee all that thou requirest: for all the city of my people doth know that thou art a virtuous woman.

1 SAMUEL 22:23

Abide thou with me, fear not: for he that seeketh my life seeketh thy life: but with me thou shalt be in safeguard.

GENESIS 43:23

And he said, Peace be to you, fear not: your God, and the God of your father, hath given you treasure in your sacks: I had your money. And he brought Simeon out unto them.

JEREMIAH 42:11

Be not afraid of the king of Babylon, of whom ye are afraid; be not afraid of him, saith the Lord: for I am with you to save you, and to deliver you from his hand.

Part I

Renewed Mind

PSALMS 51:10

> Create in me a clean heart, O God; and renew a right spirit within me.

PSALMS 119:105

> Thy word is a lamp unto my feet, and a light unto my path.

COLOSSIANS 3:1-3

> If ye then be risen with Christ, seek those things which are above, where Christ sitteth on the right hand of God.
>
> Set your affection on things above, not on things on the earth.
>
> For ye are dead, and your life is hid with Christ in God.

PSALMS 77:12

> I will meditate also of all thy work, and talk of thy doings.

PSALMS 119:48-50

> My hands also will I lift up unto thy commandments, which I have loved; and I will meditate in thy statutes.
>
> Remember the word unto thy servant, upon which thou hast caused me to hope.
>
> This is my comfort in my affliction: for thy word hath quickened me.

Knowing His Promises

JOSHUA 1:8

This book of the law shall not depart out of thy mouth; but thou shalt meditate therein day and night, that thou mayest observe to do according to all that is written therein: for then thou shalt make thy way prosperous, and then thou shalt have good success.

EPHESIANS 4:17-23

This I say therefore, and testify in the Lord, that ye henceforth walk not as other Gentiles walk, in the vanity of their mind,

Having the understanding darkened, being alienated from the life of God through the ignorance that is in them, because of the blindness of their heart:

Who being past feeling have given themselves over unto lasciviousness, to work all uncleanness with greediness.

But ye have not so learned Christ;

If so be that ye have heard him, and have been taught by him, as the truth is in Jesus:

That ye put off concerning the former conversation the old man, which is corrupt according to the deceitful lusts;

And be renewed in the spirit of your mind;

JEREMIAH 17:14-15

Heal me, O Lord, and I shall be healed; save me, and I shall be saved: for thou art my praise.

Behold, they say unto me, Where is the word of the Lord? let it come now.

Part 1 • Sound Mind • *Renewed Mind*

ROMANS 6:1-4

What shall we say then? Shall we continue in sin, that grace may abound?

God forbid. How shall we, that are dead to sin, live any longer therein?

Know ye not, that so many of us as were baptized into Jesus Christ were baptized into his death?

Therefore we are buried with him by baptism into death: that like as Christ was raised up from the dead by the glory of the Father, even so we also should walk in newness of life.

PSALMS 119:15-16

I will meditate in thy precepts, and have respect unto thy ways.

I will delight myself in thy statutes: I will not forget thy word.

ISAIAH 1:16-19

Wash you, make you clean; put away the evil of your doings from before mine eyes; cease to do evil;

Learn to do well; seek judgment, relieve the oppressed, judge the fatherless, plead for the widow.

Come now, and let us reason together, saith the Lord: though your sins be as scarlet, they shall be as white as snow; though they be red like crimson, they shall be as wool.

If ye be willing and obedient, ye shall eat the good of the land:

Knowing His Promises

ISAIAH 55:1-3

Ho, every one that thirsteth, come ye to the waters, and he that hath no money; come ye, buy, and eat; yea, come, buy wine and milk without money and without price.

Wherefore do ye spend money for that which is not bread? and your labor for that which satisfieth not? hearken diligently unto me, and eat ye that which is good, and let your soul delight itself in fatness.

Incline your ear, and come unto me: hear, and your soul shall live; and I will make an everlasting covenant with you, even the sure mercies of David.

JEREMIAH 24:7

And I will give them an heart to know me, that I am the Lord: and they shall be my people, and I will be their God: for they shall return unto me with their whole heart.

PSALMS 119:9-11

Wherewithal shall a young man cleanse his way? by taking heed thereto according to thy word.

With my whole heart have I sought thee: O let me not wander from thy commandments.

Thy word have I hid in mine heart, that I might not sin against thee.

EZEKIEL 36:26-27

A new heart also will I give you, and a new spirit will I put within you: and I will take away the stony heart out of your flesh, and I will give you an heart of flesh.

And I will put my spirit within you, and cause you to walk in my statutes, and ye shall keep my judgments, and do them.

Part 1 • **Sound Mind** • *Renewed Mind*

1 CHRONICLES 16:11-12

Seek the Lord and his strength, seek his face continually.

Remember his marvellous works that he hath done, his wonders, and the judgments of his mouth;

JOHN 8:12

Then spake Jesus again unto them, saying, I am the light of the world: he that followeth me shall not walk in darkness, but shall have the light of life.

1 KINGS 8:58

That he may incline our hearts unto him, to walk in all his ways, and to keep his commandments, and his statutes, and his judgments, which he commanded our fathers.

PSALMS 1:1-3

Blessed is the man that walketh not in the counsel of the ungodly, nor standeth in the way of sinners, nor sitteth in the seat of the scornful.

But his delight is in the law of the Lord; and in his law doth he meditate day and night.

And he shall be like a tree planted by the rivers of water, that bringeth forth his fruit in his season; his leaf also shall not wither; and whatsoever he doeth shall prosper.

JONAH 2:8

They that observe lying vanities forsake their own mercy.

Knowing His Promises

TITUS 1:15-16

Unto the pure all things are pure: but unto them that are defiled and unbelieving is nothing pure; but even their mind and conscience is defiled.

They profess that they know God; but in works they deny him, being abominable, and disobedient, and unto every good work reprobate.

PSALMS 101:3

I will set no wicked thing before mine eyes: I hate the work of them that turn aside; it shall not cleave to me.

PSALMS 139:23-24

Search me, O God, and know my heart: try me, and know my thoughts:

And see if there be any wicked way in me, and lead me in the way everlasting.

HEBREWS 4:12

For the word of God is quick, and powerful, and sharper than any twoedged sword, piercing even to the dividing asunder of soul and spirit, and of the joints and marrow, and is a discerner of the thoughts and intents of the heart.

ROMANS 12:2

And be not conformed to this world: but be ye transformed by the renewing of your mind, that ye may prove what is that good, and acceptable, and perfect, will of God.

ISAIAH 32:17

And the work of righteousness shall be peace; and the effect of righteousness quietness and assurance for ever.

Isaiah 29:13-19

Wherefore the Lord said, Forasmuch as this people draw near me with their mouth, and with their lips do honor me, but have removed their heart far from me, and their fear toward me is taught by the precept of men;

Therefore, behold, I will proceed to do a marvellous work among this people, even a marvellous work and a wonder: for the wisdom of their wise men shall perish, and the understanding of their prudent men shall be hid. Woe unto them that seek deep to hide their counsel from the Lord, and their works are in the dark, and they say, Who seeth us? and who knoweth us?

Surely your turning of things upside down shall be esteemed as the potter's clay: for shall the work say of him that made it, He made me not? or shall the thing framed say of him that framed it, He had no understanding?

Is it not yet a very little while, and Lebanon shall be turned into a fruitful field, and the fruitful field shall be esteemed as a forest?

And in that day shall the deaf hear the words of the book, and the eyes of the blind shall see out of obscurity, and out of darkness.

The meek also shall increase their joy in the Lord, and the poor among men shall rejoice in the Holy One of Israel.

Isaiah 55:11

So shall my word be that goeth forth out of my mouth: it shall not return unto me void, but it shall accomplish that which I please, and it shall prosper in the thing whereto I sent it.

Knowing His Promises

JEREMIAH 32:38-41

And they shall be my people, and I will be their God:

And I will give them one heart, and one way, that they may fear me for ever, for the good of them, and of their children after them:

And I will make an everlasting covenant with them, that I will not turn away from them, to do them good; but I will put my fear in their hearts, that they shall not depart from me.

Yea, I will rejoice over them to do them good, and I will plant them in this land assuredly with my whole heart and with my whole soul.

PSALMS 63:6-7

When I remember thee upon my bed, and meditate on thee in the night watches.

Because thou hast been my help, therefore in the shadow of thy wings will I rejoice.

ISAIAH 64:4-5

For since the beginning of the world men have not heard, nor perceived by the ear, neither hath the eye seen, O God, beside thee, what he hath prepared for him that waiteth for him.

Thou meetest him that rejoiceth and worketh righteousness, those that remember thee in thy ways: behold, thou art wroth; for we have sinned: in those is continuance, and we shall be saved.

PSALMS 71:14-15

But I will hope continually, and will yet praise thee more and more.

My mouth shall shew forth thy righteousness and thy salvation all the day; for I know not the numbers thereof.

Part 1 • Sound Mind • *Renewed Mind*

PSALMS 23:3

He restoreth my soul: he leadeth me in the paths of right-eousness for his name's sake.

PSALMS 119:148

Mine eyes prevent the night watches, that I might medi-tate in thy word.

1 CHRONICLES 28:9

And thou, Solomon my son, know thou the God of thy father, and serve him with a perfect heart and with a willing mind: for the Lord searcheth all hearts, and understandeth all the imaginations of the thoughts: if thou seek him, he will be found of thee; but if thou for-sake him, he will cast thee off for ever.

1 CORINTHIANS 2:16

For who hath known the mind of the Lord, that he may instruct him? But we have the mind of Christ.

PSALMS 143:5-6

I remember the days of old; I meditate on all thy works; I muse on the work of thy hands.

I stretch forth my hands unto thee: my soul thirsteth after thee, as a thirsty land. Selah.

MATTHEW 13:23

But he that received seed into the good ground is he that heareth the word, and understandeth it; which also beareth fruit, and bringeth forth, some an hundredfold, some sixty, some thirty.

1 TIMOTHY 4:15

Meditate upon these things; give thyself wholly to them; that thy profiting may appear to all.

Knowing His Promises

JEREMIAH 31:33

But this shall be the covenant that I will make with the house of Israel; After those days, saith the Lord, I will put my law in their inward parts, and write it in their hearts; and will be their God, and they shall be my people.

PHILIPPIANS 4:8-9

Finally, brethren, whatsoever things are true, whatsoever things are honest, whatsoever things are just, whatsoever things are pure, whatsoever things are lovely, whatsoever things are of good report; if there be any virtue, and if there be any praise, think on these things.

Those things, which ye have both learned, and received, and heard, and seen in me, do: and the God of peace shall be with you.

ROMANS 8:5-6

For they that are after the flesh do mind the things of the flesh; but they that are after the Spirit the things of the Spirit.

For to be carnally minded is death; but to be spiritually minded is life and peace.

EXODUS 13:3

And Moses said unto the people, Remember this day, in which ye came out from Egypt, out of the house of bondage; for by strength of hand the Lord brought you out from this place: there shall no leavened bread be eaten.

JOHN 15:3

Now ye are clean through the word which I have spoken unto you.

ISAIAH 55:6-9

> Seek ye the Lord while he may be found, call ye upon him while he is near:
>
> Let the wicked forsake his way, and the unrighteous man his thoughts: and let him return unto the Lord, and he will have mercy upon him; and to our God, for he will abundantly pardon.
>
> For my thoughts are not your thoughts, neither are your ways my ways, saith the Lord.
>
> For as the heavens are higher than the earth, so are my ways higher than your ways, and my thoughts than your thoughts.

PSALMS 119:114

> Thou art my hiding place and my shield: I hope in thy word.

DEUTERONOMY 30:6

> And the Lord thy God will circumcise thine heart, and the heart of thy seed, to love the Lord thy God with all thine heart, and with all thy soul, that thou mayest live.

LUKE 24:45

> Then opened he their understanding, that they might understand the scriptures,

JOHN 1:14

> And the Word was made flesh, and dwelt among us, (and we beheld his glory, the glory as of the only begotten of the Father,) full of grace and truth.

PSALMS 56:4

> In God I will praise his word, in God I have put my trust; I will not fear what flesh can do unto me.

Knowing His Promises

PROVERBS 4:23

> Keep thy heart with all diligence; for out of it are the issues of life.

PSALMS 130:5

> I wait for the Lord, my soul doth wait, and in his word do I hope.

Part I

Encouragement

PSALMS 31:22

For I said in my haste, I am cut off from before thine eyes: nevertheless thou heardest the voice of my supplications when I cried unto thee.

JONAH 2:6

I went down to the bottoms of the mountains; the earth with her bars was about me for ever: yet hast thou brought up my life from corruption, O Lord my God.

MATTHEW 24:30-31

And then shall appear the sign of the Son of man in heaven: and then shall all the tribes of the earth mourn, and they shall see the Son of man coming in the clouds of heaven with power and great glory.

And he shall send his angels with a great sound of a trumpet, and they shall gather together his elect from the four winds, from one end of heaven to the other.

ROMANS 8:26-28

Likewise the Spirit also helpeth our infirmities: for we know not what we should pray for as we ought: but the Spirit itself maketh intercession for us with groanings which cannot be uttered.

And he that searcheth the hearts knoweth what is the mind of the Spirit, because he maketh intercession for the saints according to the will of God.

And we know that all things work together for good to them that love God, to them who are the called according to his purpose.

Knowing His Promises

LAMENTATIONS 3:33

For he doth not afflict willingly nor grieve the children of men.

ISAIAH 30:18

And therefore will the Lord wait, that he may be gracious unto you, and therefore will he be exalted, that he may have mercy upon you: for the Lord is a God of judgment: blessed are all they that wait for him.

MICAH 7:7

Therefore I will look unto the Lord; I will wait for the God of my salvation: my God will hear me.

JOHN 16:33

These things I have spoken unto you, that in me ye might have peace. In the world ye shall have tribulation: but be of good cheer; I have overcome the world.

ACTS 14:22

Confirming the souls of the disciples, and exhorting them to continue in the faith, and that we must through much tribulation enter into the kingdom of God.

ROMANS 8:18

For I reckon that the sufferings of this present time are not worthy to be compared with the glory which shall be revealed in us.

2 CORINTHIANS 4:17

For our light affliction, which is but for a moment, worketh for us a far more exceeding and eternal weight of glory;

John 16:20

Verily, verily, I say unto you, That ye shall weep and lament, but the world shall rejoice: and ye shall be sorrowful, but your sorrow shall be turned into joy.

1 Peter 5:10

But the God of all grace, who hath called us unto his eternal glory by Christ Jesus, after that ye have suffered a while, make you perfect, stablish, strengthen, settle you.

Psalms 126:5

They that sow in tears shall reap in joy.

Psalms 23:4

Yea, though I walk through the valley of the shadow of death, I will fear no evil: for thou art with me; thy rod and thy staff they comfort me.

Psalms 27:5

For in the time of trouble he shall hide me in his pavilion: in the secret of his tabernacle shall he hide me; he shall set me up upon a rock.

Psalms 46:1

God is our refuge and strength, a very present help in trouble.

Psalms 50:15

And call upon me in the day of trouble: I will deliver thee, and thou shalt glorify me.

Psalms 55:22

Cast thy burden upon the Lord, and he shall sustain thee: he shall never suffer the righteous to be moved.

Knowing His Promises

PSALMS 73:26

My flesh and my heart faileth: but God is the strength of my heart, and my portion for ever.

PSALMS 119:143

Trouble and anguish have taken hold on me: yet thy commandments are my delights.

PSALMS 138:3,7

In the day when I cried thou answeredst me, and strengthenedst me with strength in my soul.

Though I walk in the midst of trouble, thou wilt revive me: thou shalt stretch forth thine hand against the wrath of mine enemies, and thy right hand shall save me.

PSALMS 147:3

He healeth the broken in heart, and bindeth up their wounds.

ISAIAH 41:10

Fear thou not; for I am with thee: be not dismayed; for I am thy God: I will strengthen thee; yea, I will help thee; yea, I will uphold thee with the right hand of my righteousness.

ISAIAH 43:2

When thou passest through the waters, I will be with thee; and through the rivers, they shall not overflow thee: when thou walkest through the fire, thou shalt not be burned; neither shall the flame kindle upon thee.

JOHN 16:22

And ye now therefore have sorrow: but I will see you again, and your heart shall rejoice, and your joy no man taketh from you.

Part 1 • Sound Mind • *Encouragement*

MATTHEW 11:28-30

Come unto me, all ye that labor and are heavy laden, and I will give you rest.

Take my yoke upon you, and learn of me; for I am meek and lowly in heart: and ye shall find rest unto your souls.

For my yoke is easy, and my burden is light.

LUKE 6:21

Blessed are ye that hunger now: for ye shall be filled. Blessed are ye that weep now: for ye shall laugh.

JOHN 14:18

I will not leave you comfortless: I will come to you.

ROMANS 8:28,35

And we know that all things work together for good to them that love God, to them who are the called according to his purpose.

Who shall separate us from the love of Christ? shall tribulation, or distress, or persecution, or famine, or nakedness, or peril, or sword?

ROMANS 12:12

Rejoicing in hope; patient in tribulation; continuing instant in prayer;

2 CORINTHIANS 1:3

Blessed be God, even the Father of our Lord Jesus Christ, the Father of mercies, and the God of all comfort;

Knowing His Promises

2 CORINTHIANS 12:19

Again, think ye that we excuse ourselves unto you? we speak before God in Christ: but we do all things, dearly beloved, for your edifying.

1 PETER 5:7

Casting all your care upon him; for he careth for you.

Part 2

Victory

ROMANS 8:37

> Nay, in all these things we are more than conquerors through him that loved us.

2 CORINTHIANS 10:3-5

> For though we walk in the flesh, we do not war after the flesh:

> (For the weapons of our warfare are not carnal, but mighty through God to the pulling down of strong holds;)

> Casting down imaginations, and every high thing that exalteth itself against the knowledge of God, and bringing into captivity every thought to the obedience of Christ; Nay, in all these things we are more than conquerors through him that loved us.

REVELATION 3:5,21

> He that overcometh, the same shall be clothed in white raiment; and I will not blot out his name out of the book of life, but I will confess his name before my Father, and before his angels.

> To him that overcometh will I grant to sit with me in my throne, even as I also overcame, and am set down with my Father in his throne.

REVELATION 21:7

> He that overcometh shall inherit all things; and I will be his God, and he shall be my son.

Knowing His Promises

1 PETER 2:11

Dearly beloved, I beseech you as strangers and pilgrims, abstain from fleshly lusts, which war against the soul;

GALATIANS 5:16,24-25

This I say then, Walk in the Spirit, and ye shall not fulfill the lust of the flesh.

And they that are Christ's have crucified the flesh with the affections and lusts.

If we live in the Spirit, let us also walk in the Spirit.

1 JOHN 5:4-5

For whatsoever is born of God overcometh the world: and this is the victory that overcometh the world, even our faith.

Who is he that overcometh the world, but he that believeth that Jesus is the Son of God?

1 CORINTHIANS 16:13

Watch ye, stand fast in the faith, quit you like men, be strong.

1 PETER 5:8-9

Be sober, be vigilant; because your adversary the devil, as a roaring lion, walketh about, seeking whom he may devour:

Whom resist stedfast in the faith, knowing that the same afflictions are accomplished in your brethren that are in the world.

HEBREWS 10:23

Let us hold fast the profession of our faith without wavering; (for he is faithful that promised;)

1 CORINTHIANS 9:25-27

And every man that striveth for the mastery is temperate
in all things. Now they do it to obtain a corruptible
crown; but we an incorruptible.

I therefore so run, not as uncertainly; so fight I, not as
one that beateth the air:

But I keep under my body, and bring it into subjection:
lest that by any means, when I have preached to others, I
myself should be a castaway.

PSALMS 27:1

The Lord is my light and my salvation; whom shall I
fear? the Lord is the strength of my life; of whom shall I
be afraid?

2 TIMOTHY 2:4

No man that warreth entangleth himself with the affairs
of this life; that he may please him who hath chosen him
to be a soldier.

JEREMIAH 9:3

And they bend their tongues like their bow for lies: but
they are not valiant for the truth upon the earth; for they
proceed from evil to evil, and they know not me, saith
the Lord.

JUDE 1:3

Beloved, when I gave all diligence to write unto you of
the common salvation, it was needful for me to write
unto you, and exhort you that ye should earnestly con-
tend for the faith which was once delivered unto the
saints.

Knowing His Promises

EPHESIANS 6:13-18

Wherefore take unto you the whole armor of God, that ye may be able to withstand in the evil day, and having done all, to stand.

Stand therefore, having your loins girt about with truth, and having on the breastplate of righteousness;

And your feet shod with the preparation of the gospel of peace;
Above all, taking the shield of faith, wherewith ye shall be able to quench all the fiery darts of the wicked.

And take the helmet of salvation, and the sword of the Spirit, which is the word of God:

Praying always with all prayer and supplication in the Spirit, and watching thereunto with all perseverance and supplication for all saints;

1 JOHN 4:4

Ye are of God, little children, and have overcome them: because greater is he that is in you, than he that is in the world.

ISAIAH 41:13-14

For I the Lord thy God will hold thy right hand, saying unto thee, Fear not; I will help thee.

Fear not, thou worm Jacob, and ye men of Israel; I will help thee, saith the Lord, and thy redeemer, the Holy One of Israel.

PSALMS 27:14

Wait on the Lord: be of good courage, and he shall strengthen thine heart: wait, I say, on the Lord.

Part 2 • **Oh My Soul** • *Victory*

ISAIAH 41:10

> Fear thou not; for I am with thee: be not dismayed; for I am thy God: I will strengthen thee; yea, I will help thee; yea, I will uphold thee with the right hand of my righteousness.

2 CORINTHIANS 12:9

> To another faith by the same Spirit; to another the gifts of healing by the same Spirit;

2 TIMOTHY 4:18

> And the Lord shall deliver me from every evil work, and will preserve me unto his heavenly kingdom: to whom be glory for ever and ever. Amen.

ROMANS 8:1-2,5-6

> There is therefore now no condemnation to them which are in Christ Jesus, who walk not after the flesh, but after the Spirit.

> For the law of the Spirit of life in Christ Jesus hath made me free from the law of sin and death.

> For they that are after the flesh do mind the things of the flesh; but they that are after the Spirit the things of the Spirit.

> For to be carnally minded is death; but to be spiritually minded is life and peace.

1 CORINTHIANS 15:57

> But thanks be to God, which giveth us the victory through our Lord Jesus Christ.

2 CORINTHIANS 2:14

> Now thanks be unto God, which always causeth us to triumph in Christ, and maketh manifest the savor of his knowledge by us in every place.

67

VICTORY

Knowing His Promises

ROMANS 13:12-14

The night is far spent, the day is at hand: let us therefore cast off the works of darkness, and let us put on the armor of light.

Let us walk honestly, as in the day; not in rioting and drunkenness, not in chambering and wantonness, not in strife and envying.

But put ye on the Lord Jesus Christ, and make not provision for the flesh, to fulfill the lusts thereof.

REVELATION 12:11

And they overcame him by the blood of the Lamb, and by the word of their testimony; and they loved not their lives unto the death.

HEBREWS 11:33-34

Who through faith subdued kingdoms, wrought righteousness, obtained promises, stopped the mouths of lions.

Quenched the violence of fire, escaped the edge of the sword, out of weakness were made strong, waxed valiant in fight, turned to flight the armies of the aliens.

ROMANS 16:20

And the God of peace shall bruise Satan under your feet shortly. The grace of our Lord Jesus Christ be with you. Amen.

ROMANS 12:21

Be not overcome of evil, but overcome evil with good.

2 TIMOTHY 2:22

Flee also youthful lusts: but follow righteousness, faith, charity, peace, with them that call on the Lord out of a pure heart.

Part 2 • Oh My Soul • *Victory*

1 JOHN 2:14-17

I have written unto you, fathers, because ye have known him that is from the beginning. I have written unto you, young men, because ye are strong, and the word of God abideth in you, and ye have overcome the wicked one.

Love not the world, neither the things that are in the world. If any man love the world, the love of the Father is not in him.

For all that is in the world, the lust of the flesh, and the lust of the eyes, and the pride of life, is not of the Father, but is of the world.
And the world passeth away, and the lust thereof: but he that doeth the will of God abideth for ever.

1 PETER 1:13-14

Wherefore gird up the loins of your mind, be sober, and hope to the end for the grace that is to be brought unto you at the revelation of Jesus Christ;

As obedient children, not fashioning yourselves according to the former lusts in your ignorance:

ROMANS 6:12-14

Let not sin therefore reign in your mortal body, that ye should obey it in the lusts thereof.

Neither yield ye your members as instruments of unrighteousness unto sin: but yield yourselves unto God, as those that are alive from the dead, and your members as instruments of righteousness unto God.

For sin shall not have dominion over you: for ye are not under the law, but under grace.

VICTORY

Knowing His Promises

EPHESIANS 4:22-23

That ye put off concerning the former conversation the old man, which is corrupt according to the deceitful lusts;

And be renewed in the spirit of your mind;

I THESSALONIANS 4:3-5

For this is the will of God, even your sanctification, that ye should abstain from fornication:

That every one of you should know how to possess his vessel in sanctification and honor;

Not in the lust of concupiscence, even as the Gentiles which know not God:

TITUS 2:12

Teaching us that, denying ungodliness and worldly lusts, we should live soberly, righteously, and godly, in this present world;

JOHN 8:32,34-36

And ye shall know the truth, and the truth shall make you free.

Jesus answered them, Verily, verily, I say unto you, Whosoever committeth sin is the servant of sin.

And the servant abideth not in the house for ever: but the Son abideth ever.

If the Son therefore shall make you free, ye shall be free indeed.

Courage

PROVERBS 28:1

The wicked flee when no man pursueth: but the righteous are bold as a lion.

EZEKIEL 2:6

And thou, son of man, be not afraid of them, neither be afraid of their words, though briers and thorns be with thee, and thou dost dwell among scorpions: be not afraid of their words, nor be dismayed at their looks, though they be a rebellious house.

EZEKIEL 3:9

As an adamant harder than flint have I made thy forehead: fear them not, neither be dismayed at their looks, though they be a rebellious house.

PHILIPPIANS 1:27-28

Only let your conversation be as it becometh the gospel of Christ: that whether I come and see you, or else be absent, I may hear of your affairs, that ye stand fast in one spirit, with one mind striving together for the faith of the gospel;

And in nothing terrified by your adversaries: which is to them an evident token of perdition, but to you of salvation, and that of God.

2 TIMOTHY 1:7

Desiring to be teachers of the law; understanding neither what they say, nor whereof they affirm.

Knowing His Promises

1 SAMUEL 17:45-51

Then said David to the Philistine, Thou comest to me with a sword, and with a spear, and with a shield: but I come to thee in the name of the Lord of hosts, the God of the armies of Israel, whom thou hast defied.

This day will the Lord deliver thee into mine hand; and I will smite thee, and take thine head from thee; and I will give the carcases of the host of the Philistines this day unto the fowls of the air, and to the wild beasts of the earth; that all the earth may know that there is a God in Israel.

And all this assembly shall know that the Lord saveth not with sword and spear: for the battle is the Lord's, and he will give you into our hands.

And it came to pass, when the Philistine arose, and came, and drew nigh to meet David, that David hastened, and ran toward the army to meet the Philistine.

And David put his hand in his bag, and took thence a stone, and slang it, and smote the Philistine in his forehead, that the stone sunk into his forehead; and he fell upon his face to the earth.

So David prevailed over the Philistine with a sling and with a stone, and smote the Philistine, and slew him; but there was no sword in the hand of David.

Therefore David ran, and stood upon the Philistine, and took his sword, and drew it out of the sheath thereof, and slew him, and cut off his head therewith. And when the Philistines saw their champion was dead, they fled.

2 CHRONICLES 13:18

Thus the children of Israel were brought under at that time, and the children of Judah prevailed, because they relied upon the Lord God of their fathers.

1 CHRONICLES 28:20

And David said to Solomon his son, Be strong and of good courage, and do it: fear not, nor be dismayed: for the Lord God, even my God, will be with thee; he will not fail thee, nor forsake thee, until thou hast finished all the work for the service of the house of the Lord.

2 CHRONICLES 32:7-8

Be strong and courageous, be not afraid nor dismayed for the king of Assyria, nor for all the multitude that is with him: for there be more with us than with him:

With him is an arm of flesh; but with us is the Lord our God to help us, and to fight our battles. And the people rested themselves upon the words of Hezekiah king of Judah.

PSALMS 18:17

He delivered me from my strong enemy, and from them which hated me: for they were too strong for me.

PSALMS 27:14

Wait on the Lord: be of good courage, and he shall strengthen thine heart: wait, I say, on the Lord.

PSALMS 31:24

Be of good courage, and he shall strengthen your heart, all ye that hope in the Lord.

ISAIAH 35:4

Say to them that are of a fearful heart, Be strong, fear not: behold, your God will come with vengeance, even God with a recompence; he will come and save you.

COURAGE

Knowing His Promises

PSALMS 89:20-24

I have found David my servant; with my holy oil have I anointed him:

With whom my hand shall be established: mine arm also shall strengthen him.

The enemy shall not exact upon him; nor the son of wickedness afflict him.

And I will beat down his foes before his face, and plague them that hate him.
But my faithfulness and my mercy shall be with him: and in my name shall his horn be exalted.

PROVERBS 24:5

A wise man is strong; yea, a man of knowledge increaseth strength.

HEBREWS 13:6

So that we may boldly say, The Lord is my helper, and I will not fear what man shall do unto me.

DEUTERONOMY 10:12

And now, Israel, what doth the Lord thy God require of thee, but to fear the Lord thy God, to walk in all his ways, and to love him, and to serve the Lord thy God with all thy heart and with all thy soul,

DEUTERONOMY 11:13

And it shall come to pass, if ye shall hearken diligently unto my commandments which I command you this day, to love the Lord your God, and to serve him with all your heart and with all your soul,

Courage

DEUTERONOMY 20:3,8

And shall say unto them, Hear, O Israel, ye approach this day unto battle against your enemies: let not your hearts faint, fear not, and do not tremble, neither be ye terrified because of them;

And the officers shall speak further unto the people, and they shall say, What man is there that is fearful and faint-hearted? let him go and return unto his house, lest his brethren's heart faint as well as his heart.

DEUTERONOMY 26:16

This day the Lord thy God hath commanded thee to do these statutes and judgments: thou shalt therefore keep and do them with all thine heart, and with all thy soul.

DEUTERONOMY 30:14

But the word is very nigh unto thee, in thy mouth, and in thy heart, that thou mayest do it.

2 CORINTHIANS 5:7

(For we walk by faith, not by sight:)

PROVERBS 14:26

In the fear of the Lord is strong confidence: and his children shall have a place of refuge.

EPHESIANS 3:16

That he would grant you, according to the riches of his glory, to be strengthened with might by his Spirit in the inner man;

MICAH 3:8

But truly I am full of power by the spirit of the Lord, and of judgment, and of might, to declare unto Jacob his transgression, and to Israel his sin.

COURAGE

Knowing His Promises

HEBREWS 11:8-9,32-34

By faith Abraham, when he was called to go out into a place which he should after receive for an inheritance, obeyed; and he went out, not knowing whither he went.

By faith he sojourned in the land of promise, as in a strange country, dwelling in tabernacles with Isaac and Jacob, the heirs with him of the same promise:

And what shall I more say? for the time would fail me to tell of Gedeon, and of Barak, and of Samson, and of Jephthae; of David also, and Samuel, and of the prophets:

Who through faith subdued kingdoms, wrought right-eousness, obtained promises, stopped the mouths of lions.

Quenched the violence of fire, escaped the edge of the sword, out of weakness were made strong, waxed valiant in fight, turned to flight the armies of the aliens.

ISAIAH 40:29,31

He giveth power to the faint; and to them that have no might he increaseth strength.

But they that wait upon the Lord shall renew their strength; they shall mount up with wings as eagles; they shall run, and not be weary; and they shall walk, and not faint.

PROVERBS 24:10

If thou faint in the day of adversity, thy strength is small.

PSALMS 29:11

The Lord will give strength unto his people; the Lord will bless his people with peace.

Part 2 • Oh My Soul • *Courage*

PSALMS 46:1

God is our refuge and strength, a very present help in trouble.

PSALMS 61:3

For thou hast been a shelter for me, and a strong tower from the enemy.

PSALMS 68:35

O God, thou art terrible out of thy holy places: the God of Israel is he that giveth strength and power unto his people. Blessed be God.

PSALMS 91:7-9,14-15

A thousand shall fall at thy side, and ten thousand at thy right hand; but it shall not come nigh thee.

Only with thine eyes shalt thou behold and see the reward of the wicked.

Because thou hast made the Lord, which is my refuge, even the most High, thy habitation;

Because he hath set his love upon me, therefore will I deliver him: I will set him on high, because he hath known my name.

He shall call upon me, and I will answer him: I will be with him in trouble; I will deliver him, and honor him. Because thou hast made the Lord, which is my refuge, even the most High, thy habitation;

PSALMS 138:3

In the day when I cried thou answeredst me, and strengthenedst me with strength in my soul.

Knowing His Promises

ISAIAH 12:2

Behold, God is my salvation; I will trust, and not be afraid: for the Lord JEHOVAH is my strength and my song; he also is become my salvation.

ACTS 4:24-31

And when they heard that, they lifted up their voice to God with one accord, and said, Lord, thou art God, which hast made heaven, and earth, and the sea, and all that in them is:

Who by the mouth of thy servant David hast said, Why did the heathen rage, and the people imagine vain things?

The kings of the earth stood up, and the rulers were gathered together against the Lord, and against his Christ.

For of a truth against thy holy child Jesus, whom thou hast anointed, both Herod, and Pontius Pilate, with the Gentiles, and the people of Israel, were gathered together,

For to do whatsoever thy hand and thy counsel determined before to be done.
And now, Lord, behold their threatenings: and grant unto thy servants, that with all boldness they may speak thy word,

By stretching forth thine hand to heal; and that signs and wonders may be done by the name of thy holy child Jesus.

And when they had prayed, the place was shaken where they were assembled together; and they were all filled with the Holy Ghost, and they spake the word of God with boldness.

EPHESIANS 1:19

And what is the exceeding greatness of his power to us-ward who believe, according to the working of his mighty power,

EPHESIANS 6:10

Finally, my brethren, be strong in the Lord, and in the power of his might.

JOSHUA 1:9

Have not I commanded thee? Be strong and of a good courage; be not afraid, neither be thou dismayed: for the Lord thy God is with thee whithersoever thou goest.

PHILIPPIANS 4:13

I can do all things through Christ which strengtheneth me.

HEBREWS 13:6

So that we may boldly say, The Lord is my helper, and I will not fear what man shall do unto me.

Part 2

Faith

1 JOHN 5:4-5

For whatsoever is born of God overcometh the world: and this is the victory that overcometh the world, even our faith.

Who is he that overcometh the world, but he that believeth that Jesus is the Son of God?

HEBREWS 11:6

But without faith it is impossible to please him: for he that cometh to God must believe that he is, and that he is a rewarder of them that diligently seek him.

ROMANS 5:2

By whom also we have access by faith into this grace wherein we stand, and rejoice in hope of the glory of God.

2 TIMOTHY 2:22

Flee also youthful lusts: but follow righteousness, faith, charity, peace, with them that call on the Lord out of a pure heart.

GALATIANS 3:26

For ye are all the children of God by faith in Christ Jesus.

HEBREWS 12:2

Looking unto Jesus the author and finisher of our faith; who for the joy that was set before him endured the

FAITH

cross, despising the shame, and is set down at the right hand of the throne of God.

JOHN 14:12

Verily, verily, I say unto you, He that believeth on me, the works that I do shall he do also; and greater works than these shall he do; because I go unto my Father.

JOHN 6:35

And Jesus said unto them, I am the bread of life: he that cometh to me shall never hunger; and he that believeth on me shall never thirst.

ROMANS 5:1

Therefore being justified by faith, we have peace with God through our Lord Jesus Christ:

ROMANS 10:17

So then faith cometh by hearing, and hearing by the word of God.

EPHESIANS 2:8-9

For by grace are ye saved through faith; and that not of yourselves: it is the gift of God:

Not of works, lest any man should boast.

GALATIANS 2:20

I am crucified with Christ: nevertheless I live; yet not I, but Christ liveth in me: and the life which I now live in the flesh I live by the faith of the Son of God, who loved me, and gave himself for me.

ACTS 14:27

> And when they were come, and had gathered the church together, they rehearsed all that God had done with them, and how he had opened the door of faith unto the Gentiles.

HEBREWS 10:22

> Let us draw near with a true heart in full assurance of faith, having our hearts sprinkled from an evil conscience, and our bodies washed with pure water.

ROMANS 1:17

> For therein is the righteousness of God revealed from faith to faith: as it is written, The just shall live by faith.

JAMES 2:17

> Even so faith, if it hath not works, is dead, being alone.

MARK 11:22-24

> And Jesus answering saith unto them, Have faith in God.
>
> For verily I say unto you, That whosoever shall say unto this mountain, Be thou removed, and be thou cast into the sea; and shall not doubt in his heart, but shall believe that those things which he saith shall come to pass; he shall have whatsoever he saith.
>
> Therefore I say unto you, What things soever ye desire, when ye pray, believe that ye receive them, and ye shall have them.

GALATIANS 2:16

> Knowing that a man is not justified by the works of the law, but by the faith of Jesus Christ, even we have believed in Jesus Christ, that we might be justified by the faith of Christ, and not by the works of the law: for by the works of the law shall no flesh be justified.

83

Knowing His Promises

JAMES 5:15

And the prayer of faith shall save the sick, and the Lord shall raise him up; and if he have committed sins, they shall be forgiven him.

HEBREWS 11:33-34

Who through faith subdued kingdoms, wrought righteousness, obtained promises, stopped the mouths of lions.

Quenched the violence of fire, escaped the edge of the sword, out of weakness were made strong, waxed valiant in fight, turned to flight the armies of the aliens.

JOHN 7:38-39

He that believeth on me, as the scripture hath said, out of his belly shall flow rivers of living water.

(But this spake he of the Spirit, which they that believe on him should receive: for the Holy Ghost was not yet given; because that Jesus was not yet glorified.)

ROMANS 4:3

For what saith the scripture? Abraham believed God, and it was counted unto him for righteousness.

MATTHEW 9:22

But Jesus turned him about, and when he saw her, he said, Daughter, be of good comfort; thy faith hath made thee whole. And the woman was made whole from that hour.

MATTHEW 21:21

Jesus answered and said unto them, Verily I say unto you, If ye have faith, and doubt not, ye shall not only do this which is done to the fig tree, but also if ye shall say unto this mountain, Be thou removed, and be thou cast into the sea; it shall be done.

Faith

GALATIANS 3:2

This only would I learn of you, Received ye the Spirit by the works of the law, or by the hearing of faith?

ACTS 15:9

And put no difference between us and them, purifying their hearts by faith.

ACTS 14:22

Confirming the souls of the disciples, and exhorting them to continue in the faith, and that we must through much tribulation enter into the kingdom of God.

JUDE 1:20-21

But ye, beloved, building up yourselves on your most holy faith, praying in the Holy Ghost,

Keep yourselves in the love of God, looking for the mercy of our Lord Jesus Christ unto eternal life.

LUKE 17:5-6

And the apostles said unto the Lord, Increase our faith.

And the Lord said, If ye had faith as a grain of mustard seed, ye might say unto this sycamine tree, Be thou plucked up by the root, and be thou planted in the sea; and it should obey you.

GALATIANS 3:11

But that no man is justified by the law in the sight of God, it is evident: for, The just shall live by faith.

HEBREWS 11:1

Now faith is the substance of things hoped for, the evidence of things not seen.

FAITH

Knowing His Promises

HABAKKUK 2:4

Behold, his soul which is lifted up is not upright in him: but the just shall live by his faith.

HEBREWS 10:38

Now the just shall live by faith: but if any man draw back, my soul shall have no pleasure in him.

ROMANS 3:28

Therefore we conclude that a man is justified by faith without the deeds of the law.

JAMES 1:6-8

But let him ask in faith, nothing wavering. For he that wavereth is like a wave of the sea driven with the wind and tossed.

For let not that man think that he shall receive any thing of the Lord.

A double minded man is unstable in all his ways.

1 CORINTHIANS 13:2,13

And though I have the gift of prophecy, and understand all mysteries, and all knowledge; and though I have all faith, so that I could remove mountains, and have not charity, I am nothing.

And now abideth faith, hope, charity, these three; but the greatest of these is charity.

HEBREW 10:23

Let us hold fast the profession of our faith without wavering; (for he is faithful that promised;)

MATTHEW 6:30

Wherefore, if God so clothe the grass of the field, which today is, and tomorrow is cast into the oven, shall he not much more clothe you, O ye of little faith?

COLOSSIANS 2:12

Buried with him in baptism, wherein also ye are risen with him through the faith of the operation of God, who hath raised him from the dead.

LUKE 22:32

But I have prayed for thee, that thy faith fail not: and when thou art converted, strengthen thy brethren.

MATTHEW 9:2

And, behold, they brought to him a man sick of the palsy, lying on a bed: and Jesus seeing their faith said unto the sick of the palsy; Son, be of good cheer; thy sins be forgiven thee.

MARK 16:17-18

And these signs shall follow them that believe; In my name shall they cast out devils; they shall speak with new tongues;

They shall take up serpents; and if they drink any deadly thing, it shall not hurt them; they shall lay hands on the sick, and they shall recover.

EPHESIANS 6:16

Above all, taking the shield of faith, wherewith ye shall be able to quench all the fiery darts of the wicked.

ROMANS 4:20

He staggered not at the promise of God through unbelief; but was strong in faith, giving glory to God;

87

Knowing His Promises

HEBREWS 11:30

By faith the walls of Jericho fell down, after they were compassed about seven days.

1 TIMOTHY 6:12

Fight the good fight of faith, lay hold on eternal life, whereunto thou art also called, and hast professed a good profession before many witnesses.

GALATIANS 5:22-23

But the fruit of the Spirit is love, joy, peace, long suffering, gentleness, goodness, faith,

Meekness, temperance: against such there is no law.

ACTS 16:5

And so were the churches established in the faith, and increased in number daily.

GALATIANS 3:22

But the scripture hath concluded all under sin, that the promise by faith of Jesus Christ might be given to them that believe.

HEBREWS 11:29

By faith they passed through the Red sea as by dry land: which the Egyptians assaying to do were drowned.

1 TIMOTHY 4:12

Let no man despise thy youth; but be thou an example of the believers, in word, in conversation, in charity, in spirit, in faith, in purity.

JAMES 2:18

Yea, a man may say, Thou hast faith, and I have works: shew me thy faith without thy works, and I will shew thee my faith by my works.

MATTHEW 9:29-30

Then touched he their eyes, saying, According to your faith be it unto you.

And their eyes were opened; and Jesus straitly charged them, saying, See that no man know it.

JAMES 1:3

Knowing this, that the trying of your faith worketh patience.

MARK 10:52

And Jesus said unto him, Go thy way; thy faith hath made thee whole. And immediately he received his sight, and followed Jesus in the way.

2 CORINTHIANS 5:7

(For we walk by faith, not by sight:)

HEBREWS 11:3

Through faith we understand that the worlds were framed by the word of God, so that things which are seen were not made of things which do appear.

MATTHEW 8:26

And he saith unto them, Why are ye fearful, O ye of little faith? Then he arose, and rebuked the winds and the sea; and there was a great calm.

Knowing His Promises

2 Thessalonians 1:11

Wherefore also we pray always for you, that our God would count you worthy of this calling, and fulfill all the good pleasure of his goodness, and the work of faith with power:

James 2:20

But wilt thou know, O vain man, that faith without works is dead?

1 Corinthians 2:5

That your faith should not stand in the wisdom of men, but in the power of God.

PART 2 • OH MY SOUL

Healing

MARK 5:35-36

> While he yet spake, there came from the ruler of the syn-
> agogue's house certain which said, Thy daughter is dead:
> why troublest thou the Master any further?
>
> As soon as Jesus heard the word that was spoken, he
> saith unto the ruler of the synagogue, Be not afraid, only
> believe.

PSALMS 107:20

> He sent his word, and healed them, and delivered them
> from their destructions.

MATTHEW 15:30

> And great multitudes came unto him, having with them
> those that were lame, blind, dumb, maimed, and many
> others, and cast them down at Jesus' feet; and he healed
> them:

LUKE 4:40

> Now when the sun was setting, all they that had any sick
> with divers diseases brought them unto him; and he laid
> his hands on every one of them, and healed them.

ACTS 5:16

> There came also a multitude out of the cities round about
> unto Jerusalem, bringing sick folks, and them which
> were vexed with unclean spirits: and they were healed
> every one.

HEALING

Knowing His Promises

JOHN 4:47-50

When he heard that Jesus was come out of Judaea into Galilee, he went unto him, and besought him that he would come down, and heal his son: for he was at the point of death.

Then said Jesus unto him, Except ye see signs and wonders, ye will not believe.

The nobleman saith unto him, Sir, come down ere my child die.

Jesus saith unto him, Go thy way; thy son liveth. And the man believed the word that Jesus had spoken unto him, and he went his way.

MATTHEW 8:13

And Jesus said unto the centurion, Go thy way; and as thou hast believed, so be it done unto thee. And his servant was healed in the selfsame hour.

MATTHEW 9:32-33

As they went out, behold, they brought to him a dumb man possessed with a devil.

And when the devil was cast out, the dumb spake: and the multitudes marvelled, saying, It was never so seen in Israel.

ACTS 28:8

And it came to pass, that the father of Publius lay sick of a fever and of a bloody flux: to whom Paul entered in, and prayed, and laid his hands on him, and healed him.

JAMES 5:14-16

> Is any sick among you? let him call for the elders of the church; and let them pray over him, anointing him with oil in the name of the Lord:
>
> And the prayer of faith shall save the sick, and the Lord shall raise him up; and if he have committed sins, they shall be forgiven him.
>
> Confess your faults one to another, and pray one for another, that ye may be healed. The effectual fervent prayer of a righteous man availeth much.

MARK 11:23-25

> For verily I say unto you, That whosoever shall say unto this mountain, Be thou removed, and be thou cast into the sea; and shall not doubt in his heart, but shall believe that those things which he saith shall come to pass; he shall have whatsoever he saith.
> Therefore I say unto you, What things soever ye desire, when ye pray, believe that ye receive them, and ye shall have them.
>
> And when ye stand praying, forgive, if ye have ought against any: that your Father also which is in heaven may forgive you your trespasses.

ROMANS 10:17

> So then faith cometh by hearing, and hearing by the word of God.

MATTHEW 9:21

> For she said within herself, If I may but touch his garment, I shall be whole.

93

Knowing His Promises

MATTHEW 12:22

Then was brought unto him one possessed with a devil, blind, and dumb: and he healed him, insomuch that the blind and dumb both spake and saw.

MARK 16:17-20

And these signs shall follow them that believe; In my name shall they cast out devils; they shall speak with new tongues;

They shall take up serpents; and if they drink any deadly thing, it shall not hurt them; they shall lay hands on the sick, and they shall recover.

So then after the Lord had spoken unto them, he was received up into heaven, and sat on the right hand of God.

And they went forth, and preached every where, the Lord working with them, and confirming the word with signs following. Amen.

PSALMS 103:2-5

Bless the Lord, O my soul, and forget not all his benefits:

Who forgiveth all thine iniquities; who healeth all thy diseases;

Who redeemeth thy life from destruction; who crowneth thee with loving kindness and tender mercies;

Who satisfieth thy mouth with good things; so that thy youth is renewed like the eagle's.

MARK 6:13

And they cast out many devils, and anointed with oil many that were sick, and healed them.

MATTHEW 9:22

But Jesus turned him about, and when he saw her, he
said, Daughter, be of good comfort; thy faith hath made
thee whole. And the woman was made whole from that
hour.

MATTHEW 12:10-13

And, behold, there was a man which had his hand with-
ered. And they asked him, saying, Is it lawful to heal on
the sabbath days? that they might accuse him.

And he said unto them, What man shall there be among
you, that shall have one sheep, and if it fall into a pit on
the sabbath day, will he not lay hold on it, and lift it out?

How much then is a man better than a sheep? Wherefore
it is lawful to do well on the sabbath days.

Then saith he to the man, Stretch forth thine hand. And
he stretched it forth; and it was restored whole, like as
the other.

ACTS 28:27

For the heart of this people is waxed gross, and their ears
are dull of hearing, and their eyes have they closed; lest
they should see with their eyes, and hear with their ears,
and understand with their heart, and should be converted,
and I should heal them.

MATTHEW 18:19-20

Again I say unto you, That if two of you shall agree on
earth as touching any thing that they shall ask, it shall be
done for them of my Father which is in heaven.

For where two or three are gathered together in my
name, there am I in the midst of them.

95

Knowing His Promises

MATTHEW 8:8

The centurion answered and said, Lord, I am not worthy that thou shouldest come under my roof: but speak the word only, and my servant shall be healed.

MATTHEW 10:1

And when he had called unto him his twelve disciples, he gave them power against unclean spirits, to cast them out, and to heal all manner of sickness and all manner of disease.

MARK 5:41-42

And he took the damsel by the hand, and said unto her, Talitha cumi; which is, being interpreted, Damsel, I say unto thee, arise.

And straightway the damsel arose, and walked; for she was of the age of twelve years. And they were astonished with a great astonishment.

MATTHEW 10:7-8

And as ye go, preach, saying, The kingdom of heaven is at hand.

Heal the sick, cleanse the lepers, raise the dead, cast out devils: freely ye have received, freely give.

LUKE 9:42

And as he was yet a coming, the devil threw him down, and tare him. And Jesus rebuked the unclean spirit, and healed the child, and delivered him again to his father.

1 PETER 2:24

Who his own self bare our sins in his own body on the tree, that we, being dead to sins, should live unto righteousness: by whose stripes ye were healed.

LUKE 17:15

And one of them, when he saw that he was healed, turned back, and with a loud voice glorified God,

MATTHEW 21:14

And the blind and the lame came to him in the temple; and he healed them.

HEBREWS 11:1

Now faith is the substance of things hoped for, the evidence of things not seen.

MATTHEW 17:18

And Jesus rebuked the devil; and he departed out of him: and the child was cured from that very hour.

LUKE 5:17

And it came to pass on a certain day, as he was teaching, that there were Pharisees and doctors of the law sitting by, which were come out of every town of Galilee, and Judaea, and Jerusalem: and the power of the Lord was present to heal them.

EXODUS 15:26

And said, If thou wilt diligently hearken to the voice of the Lord thy God, and wilt do that which is right in his sight, and wilt give ear to his commandments, and keep all his statutes, I will put none of these diseases upon thee, which I have brought upon the Egyptians: for I am the Lord that healeth thee.

MATTHEW 12:15

But when Jesus knew it, he withdrew himself from thence: and great multitudes followed him, and he healed them all;

97

Knowing His Promises

LUKE 9:2

> And he sent them to preach the kingdom of God, and to heal the sick.

MATTHEW 12:15

> But when Jesus knew it, he withdrew himself from thence: and great multitudes followed him, and he healed them all;

ACTS 4:30

> By stretching forth thine hand to heal; and that signs and wonders may be done by the name of thy holy child Jesus.

MARK 5:23

> And besought him greatly, saying, My little daughter lieth at the point of death: I pray thee, come and lay thy hands on her, that she may be healed; and she shall live.

LUKE 18:42

> And Jesus said unto him, Receive thy sight: thy faith hath saved thee.

MARK 10:52

> And Jesus said unto him, Go thy way; thy faith hath made thee whole. And immediately he received his sight, and followed Jesus in the way.

LUKE 5:15

> But so much the more went there a fame abroad of him: and great multitudes came together to hear, and to be healed by him of their infirmities.

LUKE 8:47-48

And when the woman saw that she was not hid, she came trembling, and falling down before him, she declared unto him before all the people for what cause she had touched him, and how she was healed immediately.

And he said unto her, Daughter, be of good comfort: thy faith hath made thee whole; go in peace.

ISAIAH 53:5

But he was wounded for our transgressions, he was bruised for our iniquities: the chastisement of our peace was upon him; and with his stripes we are healed.

JOHN 15:7

If ye abide in me, and my words abide in you, ye shall ask what ye will, and it shall be done unto you.

2 KINGS 20:5

Turn again, and tell Hezekiah the captain of my people, Thus saith the Lord, the God of David thy father, I have heard thy prayer, I have seen thy tears: behold, I will heal thee: on the third day thou shalt go up unto the house of the Lord.

MATTHEW 9:28-30

And when he was come into the house, the blind men came to him: and Jesus saith unto them, Believe ye that I am able to do this? They said unto him, Yea, Lord.

Then touched he their eyes, saying, According to your faith be it unto you.

And their eyes were opened; and Jesus straitly charged them, saying, See that no man know it.

VICTORY

Part 2

PART 2 • OH MY SOUL

Strength

ROMANS 14:4

Who art thou that judgest another man's servant? to his own master he standeth or falleth. Yea, he shall be holden up: for God is able to make him stand.

COLOSSIANS 1:11-12

Strengthened with all might, according to his glorious power, unto all patience and long suffering with joyfulness;

Giving thanks unto the Father, which hath made us meet to be partakers of the inheritance of the saints in light:

PSALMS 105:4

Seek the Lord, and his strength: seek his face evermore.

1 SAMUEL 2:4

The bows of the mighty men are broken, and they that stumbled are girded with strength.

EXODUS 33:16

For wherein shall it be known here that I and thy people have found grace in thy sight? is it not in that thou goest with us? so shall we be separated, I and thy people, from all the people that are upon the face of the earth.

PHILIPPIANS 1:6

Being confident of this very thing, that he which hath begun a good work in you will perform it until the day of Jesus Christ:

STRENGTH

Knowing His Promises

ACTS 20:32

And now, brethren, I commend you to God, and to the word of his grace, which is able to build you up, and to give you an inheritance among all them which are sanctified.

PSALMS 73:26

My flesh and my heart faileth: but God is the strength of my heart, and my portion for ever.

DEUTERONOMY 33:25

Thy shoes shall be iron and brass; and as thy days, so shall thy strength be.

ZECHARIAH 12:8

In that day shall the Lord defend the inhabitants of Jerusalem; and he that is feeble among them at that day shall be as David; and the house of David shall be as God, as the angel of the Lord before them.

2 PETER 1:2-4

Grace and peace be multiplied unto you through the knowledge of God, and of Jesus our Lord,

According as his divine power hath given unto us all things that pertain unto life and godliness, through the knowledge of him that hath called us to glory and virtue:

Whereby are given unto us exceeding great and precious promises: that by these ye might be partakers of the divine nature, having escaped the corruption that is in the world through lust.

JUDE 1:24

Now unto him that is able to keep you from falling, and to present you faultless before the presence of his glory with exceeding joy,

PSALMS 30:7

> Lord, by thy favor thou hast made my mountain to stand strong: thou didst hide thy face, and I was troubled.

JOHN 1:16

> And of his fulness have all we received, and grace for grace.

PSALMS 29:11

> The Lord will give strength unto his people; the Lord will bless his people with peace.

2 CORINTHIANS 10:4

> (For the weapons of our warfare are not carnal, but mighty through God to the pulling down of strong holds;)

PSALMS 18:35-36

> Thou hast also given me the shield of thy salvation: and thy right hand hath holden me up, and thy gentleness hath made me great.
>
> Thou hast enlarged my steps under me, that my feet did not slip.

ISAIAH 45:24

> Surely, shall one say, in the Lord have I righteousness and strength: even to him shall men come; and all that are incensed against him shall be ashamed.

PSALMS 37:24

> Though he fall, he shall not be utterly cast down: for the Lord upholdeth him with his hand.

Knowing His Promises

1 JOHN 4:4

Ye are of God, little children, and have overcome them: because greater is he that is in you, than he that is in the world.

PHILIPPIANS 4:7

And the peace of God, which passeth all understanding, shall keep your hearts and minds through Christ Jesus.

MALACHI 4:2

But unto you that fear my name shall the Sun of righteousness arise with healing in his wings; and ye shall go forth, and grow up as calves of the stall.

ISAIAH 41:13-14

For I the Lord thy God will hold thy right hand, saying unto thee, Fear not; I will help thee.

Fear not, thou worm Jacob, and ye men of Israel; I will help thee, saith the Lord, and thy redeemer, the Holy One of Israel.

PSALMS 71:16

I will go in the strength of the Lord God: I will make mention of thy righteousness, even of thine only.

2 CORINTHIANS 9:8

And God is able to make all grace abound toward you; that ye, always having all sufficiency in all things, may abound to every good work:

DEUTERONOMY 33:27

The eternal God is thy refuge, and underneath are the everlasting arms: and he shall thrust out the enemy from before thee; and shall say, Destroy them.

Part 2 • Oh My Soul • *Strength*

JAMES 1:17

Every good gift and every perfect gift is from above, and
cometh down from the Father of lights, with whom is no
variableness, neither shadow of turning.

ISAIAH 33:5-6

The Lord is exalted; for he dwelleth on high: he hath
filled Zion with judgment and righteousness.

And wisdom and knowledge shall be the stability of thy
times, and strength of salvation: the fear of the Lord is
his treasure.

PSALMS 1:3

And he shall be like a tree planted by the rivers of water,
that bringeth forth his fruit in his season; his leaf also
shall not wither; and whatsoever he doeth shall prosper.

PSALMS 94:17-18

Unless the Lord had been my help, my soul had almost
dwelt in silence.

When I said, My foot slippeth; thy mercy, O Lord, held
me up.

PROVERBS 10:29

The way of the Lord is strength to the upright: but
destruction shall be to the workers of iniquity.

NEHEMIAH 8:10

Then he said unto them, Go your way, eat the fat, and
drink the sweet, and send portions unto them for whom
nothing is prepared: for this day is holy unto our Lord:
neither be ye sorry; for the joy of the Lord is your
strength.

STRENGTH

Knowing His Promises

GENESIS 49:24

But his bow abode in strength, and the arms of his hands were made strong by the hands of the mighty God of Jacob; (from thence is the shepherd, the stone of Israel:)

PSALMS 84:4

Blessed are they that dwell in thy house: they will be still praising thee. Selah.

PSALMS 23:2-3

He maketh me to lie down in green pastures: he leadeth me beside the still waters.

He restoreth my soul: he leadeth me in the paths of righteousness for his name's sake.

HABAKKUK 3:19

The Lord God is my strength, and he will make my feet like hinds' feet, and he will make me to walk upon mine high places. To the chief singer on my stringed instruments.

PSALMS 18:1-2

I will love thee, O Lord, my strength.

The Lord is my rock, and my fortress, and my deliverer; my God, my strength, in whom I will trust; my buckler, and the horn of my salvation, and my high tower.

EXODUS 15:2

The Lord is my strength and song, and he is become my salvation: he is my God, and I will prepare him an habitation; my father's God, and I will exalt him.

PSALMS 144:1-2

Blessed be the Lord my strength which teacheth my hands to war, and my fingers to fight:

My goodness, and my fortress; my high tower, and my deliverer; my shield, and he in whom I trust; who subdueth my people under me.

PSALMS 66:9

Which holdeth our soul in life, and suffereth not our feet to be moved.

PSALMS 37:17

For the arms of the wicked shall be broken: but the Lord upholdeth the righteous.

JEREMIAH 31:14

And I will satiate the soul of the priests with fatness, and my people shall be satisfied with my goodness, saith the Lord.

DANIEL 11:32

And such as do wickedly against the covenant shall he corrupt by flatteries: but the people that do know their God shall be strong, and do exploits.

PHILIPPIANS 4:19

But my God shall supply all your need according to his riches in glory by Christ Jesus.

JOB 23:6

Will he plead against me with his great power? No; but he would put strength in me.

Knowing His Promises

PSALMS 68:35

O God, thou art terrible out of thy holy places: the God of Israel is he that giveth strength and power unto his people. Blessed be God.

PSALMS 68:35

O God, thou art terrible out of thy holy places: the God of Israel is he that giveth strength and power unto his people. Blessed be God.

PSALMS 37:39

But the salvation of the righteous is of the Lord: he is their strength in the time of trouble.

EPHESIANS 3:20

Now unto him that is able to do exceeding abundantly above all that we ask or think, according to the power that worketh in us,

I THESSALONIANS 5:24

Faithful is he that calleth you, who also will do it.

PSALMS 68:28

Thy God hath commanded thy strength: strengthen, O God, that which thou hast wrought for us.

PSALMS 146:5

Happy is he that hath the God of Jacob for his help, whose hope is in the Lord his God:

PSALMS 138:8

The Lord will perfect that which concerneth me; thy mercy, O Lord, endureth for ever: forsake not the works of thine own hands.

ISAIAH 54:17

No weapon that is formed against thee shall prosper; and every tongue that shall rise against thee in judgment thou shalt condemn. This is the heritage of the servants of the Lord, and their righteousness is of me, saith the Lord.

PSALMS 89:17

For thou art the glory of their strength: and in thy favor our horn shall be exalted.

ZECHARIAH 10:12

And I will strengthen them in the Lord; and they shall walk up and down in his name, saith the Lord.

ISAIAH 40:29

He giveth power to the faint; and to them that have no might he increaseth strength.

PSALMS 55:22

Cast thy burden upon the Lord, and he shall sustain thee: he shall never suffer the righteous to be moved.

ISAIAH 41:10

Fear thou not; for I am with thee: be not dismayed; for I am thy God: I will strengthen thee; yea, I will help thee; yea, I will uphold thee with the right hand of my righteousness.

PSALMS 28:8

The Lord is their strength, and he is the saving strength of his anointed.

Knowing His Promises

PSALMS 27:14

Wait on the Lord: be of good courage, and he shall strengthen thine heart: wait, I say, on the Lord.

PSALMS 63:8

My soul followeth hard after thee: thy right hand upholdeth me.

ISAIAH 40:31

But they that wait upon the Lord shall renew their strength; they shall mount up with wings as eagles; they shall run, and not be weary; and they shall walk, and not faint.

2 CORINTHIANS 3:5

Not that we are sufficient of ourselves to think any thing as of ourselves; but our sufficiency is of God;

PSALMS 138:3

In the day when I cried thou answeredst me, and strengthenedst me with strength in my soul.

PHILIPPIANS 2:13

For it is God which worketh in you both to will and to do of his good pleasure.

PSALMS 84:11

For the Lord God is a sun and shield: the Lord will give grace and glory: no good thing will he withhold from them that walk uprightly.

PSALMS 31:24

Be of good courage, and he shall strengthen your heart, all ye that hope in the Lord.

Witnessing

JOHN 6:37,44-45

All that the Father giveth me shall come to me; and him that cometh to me I will in no wise cast out.

No man can come to me, except the Father which hath sent me draw him: and I will raise him up at the last day.

It is written in the prophets, And they shall be all taught of God. Every man therefore that hath heard, and hath learned of the Father, cometh unto me.

ROMANS 1:16-17

For I am not ashamed of the gospel of Christ: for it is the power of God unto salvation to every one that believeth; to the Jew first, and also to the Greek.

For therein is the righteousness of God revealed from faith to faith: as it is written, The just shall live by faith.

REVELATION 3:20

Behold, I stand at the door, and knock: if any man hear my voice, and open the door, I will come in to him, and will sup with him, and he with me.

1 JOHN 5:11-13

And this is the record, that God hath given to us eternal life, and this life is in his Son.

He that hath the Son hath life; and he that hath not the Son of God hath not life.

Knowing His Promises

These things have I written unto you that believe on the name of the Son of God; that ye may know that ye have eternal life, and that ye may believe on the name of the Son of God.

1 JOHN 4:9-10

In this was manifested the love of God toward us, because that God sent his only begotten Son into the world, that we might live through him.

Herein is love, not that we loved God, but that he loved us, and sent his Son to be the propitiation for our sins.

HEBREWS 2:3

How shall we escape, if we neglect so great salvation; which at the first began to be spoken by the Lord, and was confirmed unto us by them that heard him;

EPHESIANS 2:9-10

Not of works, lest any man should boast.

For we are his workmanship, created in Christ Jesus unto good works, which God hath before ordained that we should walk in them.

EPHESIANS 6:19

And for me, that utterance may be given unto me, that I may open my mouth boldly, to make known the mystery of the gospel,

ROMANS 10:9-10

That if thou shalt confess with thy mouth the Lord Jesus, and shalt believe in thine heart that God hath raised him from the dead, thou shalt be saved.

For with the heart man believeth unto righteousness; and with the mouth confession is made unto salvation.

ROMANS 3:23

For all have sinned, and come short of the glory of God;

ACTS 16:30-31

And brought them out, and said, Sirs, what must I do to be saved?

And they said, Believe on the Lord Jesus Christ, and thou shalt be saved, and thy house.

ACTS 4:12

Neither is there salvation in any other: for there is none other name under heaven given among men, whereby we must be saved.

JOHN 15:4-5

Abide in me, and I in you. As the branch cannot bear fruit of itself, except it abide in the vine; no more can ye, except ye abide in me.

I am the vine, ye are the branches: He that abideth in me, and I in him, the same bringeth forth much fruit: for without me ye can do nothing.

JOHN 3:16-17

For God so loved the world, that he gave his only begotten Son, that whosoever believeth in him should not perish, but have everlasting life.

For God sent not his Son into the world to condemn the world; but that the world through him might be saved.

PROVERBS 11:30

The fruit of the righteous is a tree of life; and he that winneth souls is wise.

Knowing His Promises

MATTHEW 28:19-20

> Go ye therefore, and teach all nations, baptizing them in the name of the Father, and of the Son, and of the Holy Ghost:

> Teaching them to observe all things whatsoever I have commanded you: and, lo, I am with you always, even unto the end of the world. Amen.

PSALMS 96:2-3,10

> Sing unto the Lord, bless his name; shew forth his salvation from day to day.

> Declare his glory among the heathen, his wonders among all people.

> Say among the heathen that the Lord reigneth: the world also shall be established that it shall not be moved: he shall judge the people righteously.

ISAIAH 52:7

> How beautiful upon the mountains are the feet of him that bringeth good tidings, that publisheth peace; that bringeth good tidings of good, that publisheth salvation; that saith unto Zion, Thy God reigneth!

MATTHEW 5:16

> Let your light so shine before men, that they may see your good works, and glorify your Father which is in heaven.

LUKE 8:16

> No man, when he hath lighted a candle, covereth it with a vessel, or putteth it under a bed; but setteth it on a candlestick, that they which enter in may see the light.

ACTS 10:42

And he commanded us to preach unto the people, and to testify that it is he which was ordained of God to be the Judge of quick and dead.

EPHESIANS 5:15-16

See then that ye walk circumspectly, not as fools, but as wise,

Redeeming the time, because the days are evil.

EPHESIANS 6:14-20

Stand therefore, having your loins girt about with truth, and having on the breastplate of righteousness;

And your feet shod with the preparation of the gospel of peace;

Above all, taking the shield of faith, wherewith ye shall be able to quench all the fiery darts of the wicked.

And take the helmet of salvation, and the sword of the Spirit, which is the word of God:

Praying always with all prayer and supplication in the Spirit, and watching thereunto with all perseverance and supplication for all saints;

And for me, that utterance may be given unto me, that I may open my mouth boldly, to make known the mystery of the gospel,

For which I am an ambassador in bonds: that therein I may speak boldly, as I ought to speak.

Knowing His Promises

PHILIPPIANS 1:27-28

Only let your conversation be as it becometh the gospel of Christ: that whether I come and see you, or else be absent, I may hear of your affairs, that ye stand fast in one spirit, with one mind striving together for the faith of the gospel;

And in nothing terrified by your adversaries: which is to them an evident token of perdition, but to you of salvation, and that of God.

COLOSSIANS 4:5-6

Walk in wisdom toward them that are without, redeeming the time.

Let your speech be always with grace, seasoned with salt, that ye may know how ye ought to answer every man.

JAMES 5:20

Let him know, that he which converteth the sinner from the error of his way shall save a soul from death, and shall hide a multitude of sins.

GALATIANS 6:9

And let us not be weary in well doing: for in due season we shall reap, if we faint not.

MATTHEW 11:28-30

Come unto me, all ye that labor and are heavy laden, and I will give you rest.

Take my yoke upon you, and learn of me; for I am meek and lowly in heart: and ye shall find rest unto your souls.

For my yoke is easy, and my burden is light.

Part 2 • **Oh My Soul** • *Witnessing*

REVELATION 22:17

> And the Spirit and the bride say, Come. And let him that heareth say, Come. And let him that is athirst come. And whosoever will, let him take the water of life freely.

ROMANS 6:23

> For the wages of sin is death; but the gift of God is eternal life through Jesus Christ our Lord.

JOHN 5:24

> Verily, verily, I say unto you, He that heareth my word, and believeth on him that sent me, hath everlasting life, and shall not come into condemnation; but is passed from death unto life.

JOHN 6:27-29,40,47

> Labor not for the meat which perisheth, but for that meat which endureth unto everlasting life, which the Son of man shall give unto you: for him hath God the Father sealed.

> Then said they unto him, What shall we do, that we might work the works of God?

> Jesus answered and said unto them, This is the work of God, that ye believe on him whom he hath sent.

> And this is the will of him that sent me, that every one which seeth the Son, and believeth on him, may have everlasting life: and I will raise him up at the last day.

> Verily, verily, I say unto you, He that believeth on me hath everlasting life.

117

Knowing His Promises

JOHN 10:10-14,27-28

The thief cometh not, but for to steal, and to kill, and to destroy: I am come that they might have life, and that they might have it more abundantly.

I am the good shepherd: the good shepherd giveth his life for the sheep.

But he that is an hireling, and not the shepherd, whose own the sheep are not, seeth the wolf coming, and leaveth the sheep, and fleeth: and the wolf catcheth them, and scattereth the sheep.

The hireling fleeth, because he is an hireling, and careth not for the sheep.

I am the good shepherd, and know my sheep, and am known of mine.

My sheep hear my voice, and I know them, and they follow me:

And I give unto them eternal life; and they shall never perish, neither shall any man pluck them out of my hand.

PART 3 • RENEW MY SPIRIT

Salvation

ECCLESIASTES 7:20

For there is not a just man upon earth, that doeth good, and sinneth not.

ROMANS 5:12-14

Wherefore, as by one man sin entered into the world, and death by sin; and so death passed upon all men, for that all have sinned:

(For until the law sin was in the world: but sin is not imputed when there is no law.

Nevertheless death reigned from Adam to Moses, even over them that had not sinned after the similitude of Adam's transgression, who is the figure of him that was to come.

1 JOHN 2:16-17

For all that is in the world, the lust of the flesh, and the lust of the eyes, and the pride of life, is not of the Father, but is of the world.

And the world passeth away, and the lust thereof: but he that doeth the will of God abideth for ever.

ISAIAH 64:6

But we are all as an unclean thing, and all our righteous-nesses are as filthy rags; and we all do fade as a leaf; and our iniquities, like the wind, have taken us away.

SALVATION

Knowing His Promises

JOB 4:17

Shall mortal man be more just than God? shall a man be more pure than his maker?

ISAIAH 25:4

For thou hast been a strength to the poor, a strength to the needy in his distress, a refuge from the storm, a shadow from the heat, when the blast of the terrible ones is as a storm against the wall.

JOHN 6:35

And Jesus said unto them, I am the bread of life: he that cometh to me shall never hunger; and he that believeth on me shall never thirst.

JEREMIAH 13:23

Can the Ethiopian change his skin, or the leopard his spots? then may ye also do good, that are accustomed to do evil.

JEREMIAH 17:9-10

The heart is deceitful above all things, and desperately wicked: who can know it?

I the Lord search the heart, I try the reins, even to give every man according to his ways, and according to the fruit of his doings.

TITUS 3:3-5

For we ourselves also were sometimes foolish, disobedient, deceived, serving divers lusts and pleasures, living in malice and envy, hateful, and hating one another.

But after that the kindness and love of God our Savior toward man appeared,

Not by works of righteousness which we have done, but according to his mercy he saved us, by the washing of regeneration, and renewing of the Holy Ghost;

JOHN 3:19-21

And this is the condemnation, that light is come into the world, and men loved darkness rather than light, because their deeds were evil.

For every one that doeth evil hateth the light, neither cometh to the light, lest his deeds should be reproved.

But he that doeth truth cometh to the light, that his deeds may be made manifest, that they are wrought in God.

EPHESIANS 2:1-3

And you hath he quickened, who were dead in trespasses and sins;

Wherein in time past ye walked according to the course of this world, according to the prince of the power of the air, the spirit that now worketh in the children of disobedience:

Among whom also we all had our conversation in times past in the lusts of our flesh, fulfilling the desires of the flesh and of the mind; and were by nature the children of wrath, even as others.

Knowing His Promises

GALATIANS 5:19-21

Now the works of the flesh are manifest, which are these; Adultery, fornication, uncleanness, lasciviousness,

Idolatry, witchcraft, hatred, variance, emulations, wrath, strife, seditions, heresies,

Envyings, murders, drunkenness, revellings, and such like: of the which I tell you before, as I have also told you in time past, that they which do such things shall not inherit the kingdom of God.

GALATIANS 3:10-11

For as many as are of the works of the law are under the curse: for it is written, Cursed is every one that continueth not in all things which are written in the book of the law to do them.

But that no man is justified by the law in the sight of God, it is evident: for, The just shall live by faith.

JOHN 5:24

Verily, verily, I say unto you, He that heareth my word, and believeth on him that sent me, hath everlasting life, and shall not come into condemnation; but is passed from death unto life.

JOHN 8:23-24

And he said unto them, Ye are from beneath; I am from above: ye are of this world; I am not of this world.

I said therefore unto you, that ye shall die in your sins: for if ye believe not that I am he, ye shall die in your sins.

GALATIANS 3:22

But the scripture hath concluded all under sin, that the promise by faith of Jesus Christ might be given to them that believe.

1 JOHN 1:10

He was in the world, and the world was made by him, and the world knew him not.

PROVERBS 20:9

Who can say, I have made my heart clean, I am pure from my sin?

ECCLESIASTES 8:11

Because sentence against an evil work is not executed speedily, therefore the heart of the sons of men is fully set in them to do evil.

PSALMS 37:39-40

But the salvation of the righteous is of the Lord: he is their strength in the time of trouble.

And the Lord shall help them, and deliver them: he shall deliver them from the wicked, and save them, because they trust in him.

JOHN 12:46

I am come a light into the world, that whosoever believeth on me should not abide in darkness.

ROMANS 2:1

Therefore thou art inexcusable, O man, whosoever thou art that judgest: for wherein thou judgest another, thou condemnest thyself; for thou that judgest doest the same things.

JOHN 20:31

But these are written, that ye might believe that Jesus is the Christ, the Son of God; and that believing ye might have life through his name.

Salvation

SALVATION

Knowing His Promises

2 Chronicles 6:36-39

If they sin against thee, (for there is no man which sinneth not,) and thou be angry with them, and deliver them over before their enemies, and they carry them away captives unto a land far off or near;

Yet if they bethink themselves in the land whither they are carried captive, and turn and pray unto thee in the land of their captivity, saying, We have sinned, we have done amiss, and have dealt wickedly;

If they return to thee with all their heart and with all their soul in the land of their captivity, whither they have carried them captives, and pray toward their land, which thou gavest unto their fathers, and toward the city which thou hast chosen, and toward the house which I have built for thy name:

Then hear thou from the heavens, even from thy dwelling place, their prayer and their supplications, and maintain their cause, and forgive thy people which have sinned against thee.

Isaiah 53:4-6

Surely he hath born our griefs, and carried our sorrows: yet we did esteem him stricken, smitten of God, and afflicted.

But he was wounded for our transgressions, he was bruised for our iniquities: the chastisement of our peace was upon him; and with his stripes we are healed.

All we like sheep have gone astray; we have turned every one to his own way; and the Lord hath laid on him the iniquity of us all.

1 Samuel 2:2

There is none holy as the Lord: for there is none beside thee: neither is there any rock like our God.

PSALMS 130:3-4

If thou, Lord, shouldest mark iniquities, O Lord, who shall stand?

But there is forgiveness with thee, that thou mayest be feared.

JOHN 1:12-13

But as many as received him, to them gave he power to become the sons of God, even to them that believe on his name:

Which were born, not of blood, nor of the will of the flesh, nor of the will of man, but of God.

MATTHEW 11:28-30

Come unto me, all ye that labor and are heavy laden, and I will give you rest.

Take my yoke upon you, and learn of me; for I am meek and lowly in heart: and ye shall find rest unto your souls.

For my yoke is easy, and my burden is light.

ISAIAH 45:21-22

Tell ye, and bring them near; yea, let them take counsel together: who hath declared this from ancient time? who hath told it from that time? have not I the Lord? and there is no God else beside me; a just God and a Savior; there is none beside me.

Look unto me, and be ye saved, all the ends of the earth: for I am God, and there is none else.

JOHN 3:36

He that believeth on the Son hath everlasting life: and he that believeth not the Son shall not see life; but the wrath of God abideth on him.

Knowing His Promises

ROMANS 3:10-19

As it is written, There is none righteous, no, not one:

There is none that understandeth, there is none that seeketh after God.

They are all gone out of the way, they are together become unprofitable; there is none that doeth good, no, not one.

Their throat is an open sepulchre; with their tongues they have used deceit; the poison of asps is under their lips:

Whose mouth is full of cursing and bitterness:

Their feet are swift to shed blood:

Destruction and misery are in their ways:

And the way of peace have they not known:

There is no fear of God before their eyes.

Now we know that what things soever the law saith, it saith to them who are under the law: that every mouth may be stopped, and all the world may become guilty before God.

PSALMS 14:1-3

The fool hath said in his heart, There is no God. They are corrupt, they have done abominable works, there is none that doeth good.

The Lord looked down from heaven upon the children of men, to see if there were any that did understand, and seek God.

They are all gone aside, they are all together become filthy: there is none that doeth good, no, not one.

Part 3 • **Renew My Spirit** • *Salvation*

JOHN 4:42

And said unto the woman, Now we believe, not because of thy saying: for we have heard him ourselves, and know that this is indeed the Christ, the Savior of the world.

ROMANS 6:23

For the wages of sin is death; but the gift of God is eternal life through Jesus Christ our Lord.

JOHN 11:25

Jesus said unto her, I am the resurrection, and the life: he that believeth in me, though he were dead, yet shall he live:

HOSEA 13:4

Yet I am the Lord thy God from the land of Egypt, and thou shalt know no God but me: for there is no savior beside me.

1 JOHN 1:8

If we say that we have no sin, we deceive ourselves, and the truth is not in us.

ISAIAH 19:20

And it shall be for a sign and for a witness unto the Lord of hosts in the land of Egypt: for they shall cry unto the Lord because of the oppressors, and he shall send them a savior, and a great one, and he shall deliver them.

2 SAMUEL 22:3-4

The God of my rock; in him will I trust: he is my shield, and the horn of my salvation, my high tower, and my refuge, my savior; thou savest me from violence.

I will call on the Lord, who is worthy to be praised: so shall I be saved from mine enemies.

Knowing His Promises

MARK 16:16

He that believeth and is baptized shall be saved; but he that believeth not shall be damned.

MATTHEW 5:20

For I say unto you, That except your righteousness shall exceed the righteousness of the scribes and Pharisees, ye shall in no case enter into the kingdom of heaven.

ROMANS 3:23

For all have sinned, and come short of the glory of God;

ACTS 5:31

Him hath God exalted with his right hand to be a Prince and a Savior, for to give repentance to Israel, and forgiveness of sins.

ECCLESIASTES 9:3

This is an evil among all things that are done under the sun, that there is one event unto all: yea, also the heart of the sons of men is full of evil, and madness is in their heart while they live, and after that they go to the dead.

PSALMS 34:22

The Lord redeemeth the soul of his servants: and none of them that trust in him shall be desolate.

PSALMS 25:5-6

Lead me in thy truth, and teach me: for thou art the God of my salvation; on thee do I wait all the day.

Remember, O Lord, thy tender mercies and thy loving kindnesses; for they have been ever of old.

PSALMS 94:11

The Lord knoweth the thoughts of man, that they are vanity.

LAMENTATIONS 3:22

It is of the Lord's mercies that we are not consumed, because his compassions fail not.

PSALMS 33:18-19

Behold, the eye of the Lord is upon them that fear him, upon them that hope in his mercy;

To deliver their soul from death, and to keep them alive in famine.

1 PETER 1:18

Forasmuch as ye know that ye were not redeemed with corruptible things, as silver and gold, from your vain conversation received by tradition from your fathers;

JEREMIAH 2:29

Wherefore will ye plead with me? ye all have transgressed against me, saith the Lord.

EPHESIANS 4:17-19

This I say therefore, and testify in the Lord, that ye henceforth walk not as other Gentiles walk, in the vanity of their mind,

Having the understanding darkened, being alienated from the life of God through the ignorance that is in them, because of the blindness of their heart:

Who being past feeling have given themselves over unto lasciviousness, to work all uncleanness with greediness.

Knowing His Promises

JEREMIAH 2:22

For though thou wash thee with nitre, and take thee much soap, yet thine iniquity is marked before me, saith the Lord God.

1 PETER 1:18

Forasmuch as ye know that ye were not redeemed with corruptible things, as silver and gold, from your vain conversation received by tradition from your fathers;

PSALMS 68:19

Blessed be the Lord, who daily loadeth us with benefits, even the God of our salvation. Selah.

TITUS 3:4-5

But after that the kindness and love of God our Savior toward man appeared,

Not by works of righteousness which we have done, but according to his mercy he saved us, by the washing of regeneration, and renewing of the Holy Ghost;

Part 3

PART 3 • RENEW MY SPIRIT

Relationships

LEVITICUS 19:3

Ye shall fear every man his mother, and his father, and keep my sabbaths: I am the Lord your God.

DEUTERONOMY 5:16

Honor thy father and thy mother, as the Lord thy God hath commanded thee; that thy days may be prolonged, and that it may go well with thee, in the land which the Lord thy God giveth thee.

PROVERBS 1:8-9

My son, hear the instruction of thy father, and forsake not the law of thy mother:

For they shall be an ornament of grace unto thy head, and chains about thy neck.

PROVERBS 3:1-3

My son, forget not my law; but let thine heart keep my commandments:

For length of days, and long life, and peace, shall they add to thee.

Let not mercy and truth forsake thee: bind them about thy neck; write them upon the table of thine heart:

RELATIONSHIPS

Knowing His Promises

PROVERBS 4:1-4

> Hear, ye children, the instruction of a father, and attend to know understanding.
>
> For I give you good doctrine, forsake ye not my law.
>
> For I was my father's son, tender and only beloved in the sight of my mother.
>
> He taught me also, and said unto me, Let thine heart retain my words: keep my commandments, and live.

PROVERBS 6:20-25

> My son, keep thy father's commandment, and forsake not the law of thy mother:
>
> Bind them continually upon thine heart, and tie them about thy neck.
>
> When thou goest, it shall lead thee; when thou sleepest, it shall keep thee; and when thou awakest, it shall talk with thee.
>
> For the commandment is a lamp; and the law is light; and reproofs of instruction are the way of life:
>
> To keep thee from the evil woman, from the flattery of the tongue of a strange woman.
>
> Lust not after her beauty in thine heart; neither let her take thee with her eyelids.

PROVERBS 23:22

> Hearken unto thy father that begat thee, and despise not thy mother when she is old.

COLOSSIANS 3:20

> Children, obey your parents in all things: for this is well pleasing unto the Lord.

MATTHEW 15:4

For God commanded, saying, Honor thy father and mother: and, He that curseth father or mother, let him die the death.

MATTHEW 19:19

Honor thy father and thy mother: and, Thou shalt love thy neighbor as thyself.

EPHESIANS 6:1-3

Children, obey your parents in the Lord: for this is right.

Honor thy father and mother; which is the first commandment with promise;

That it may be well with thee, and thou mayest live long on the earth.

2 CORINTHIANS 6:14-17

Be ye not unequally yoked together with unbelievers: for what fellowship hath righteousness with unrighteousness? and what communion hath light with darkness?

And what concord hath Christ with Belial? or what part hath he that believeth with an infidel?

And what agreement hath the temple of God with idols? for ye are the temple of the living God; as God hath said, I will dwell in them, and walk in them; and I will be their God, and they shall be my people.

Wherefore come out from among them, and be ye separate, saith the Lord, and touch not the unclean thing; and I will receive you.

Knowing His Promises

EZRA 9:12

Now therefore give not your daughters unto their sons, neither take their daughters unto your sons, nor seek their peace or their wealth for ever: that ye may be strong, and eat the good of the land, and leave it for an inheritance to your children for ever.

DEUTERONOMY 7:3-4

Neither shalt thou make marriages with them; thy daughter thou shalt not give unto his son, nor his daughter shalt thou take unto thy son.

For they will turn away thy son from following me, that they may serve other gods: so will the anger of the Lord be kindled against you, and destroy thee suddenly.

MALACHI 2:11

Judah hath dealt treacherously, and an abomination is committed in Israel and in Jerusalem; for Judah hath profaned the holiness of the Lord which he loved, and hath married the daughter of a strange God.

1 CORINTHIANS 6:18-20

Flee fornication. Every sin that a man doeth is without the body; but he that committeth fornication sinneth against his own body.

What? know ye not that your body is the temple of the Holy Ghost which is in you, which ye have of God, and ye are not your own?

For ye are bought with a price: therefore glorify God in your body, and in your spirit, which are God's.

EXODUS 23:2,32-33

Thou shalt not follow a multitude to do evil; neither shalt thou speak in a cause to decline after many to wrest judgment:

Thou shalt make no covenant with them, nor with their gods.

They shall not dwell in thy land, lest they make thee sin against me: for if thou serve their gods, it will surely be a snare unto thee.

DEUTERONOMY 12:30

Take heed to thyself that thou be not snared by following them, after that they be destroyed from before thee; and that thou enquire not after their gods, saying, How did these nations serve their gods? even so will I do likewise.

PSALMS 26:4-5

I have not sat with vain persons, neither will I go in with dissemblers.

I have hated the congregation of evil doers; and will not sit with the wicked.

PSALMS 119:115

Depart from me, ye evildoers: for I will keep the commandments of my God.

PSALMS 141:4-5

Incline not my heart to any evil thing, to practice wicked works with men that work iniquity: and let me not eat of their dainties.

Let the righteous smite me; it shall be a kindness: and let him reprove me; it shall be an excellent oil, which shall not break my head: for yet my prayer also shall be in their calamities.

Knowing His Promises

PROVERBS 1:10,15

My son, if sinners entice thee, consent thou not.

My son, walk not thou in the way with them; refrain thy foot from their path:

PROVERBS 13:20

He that walketh with wise men shall be wise: but a companion of fools shall be destroyed.

1 CORINTHIANS 5:9-11

I wrote unto you in an epistle not to company with fornicators:

Yet not altogether with the fornicators of this world, or with the covetous, or extortioners, or with idolaters; for then must ye needs go out of the world.

But now I have written unto you not to keep company, if any man that is called a brother be a fornicator, or covetous, or an idolater, or a railer, or a drunkard, or an extortioner; with such an one no not to eat.

1 CORINTHIANS 15:33

Be not deceived: evil communications corrupt good manners.

PROVERBS 4:14-15

Enter not into the path of the wicked, and go not in the way of evil men.

Avoid it, pass not by it, turn from it, and pass away.

EPHESIANS 5:11

And have no fellowship with the unfruitful works of darkness, but rather reprove them.

2 TIMOTHY 3:25

> For men shall be lovers of their own selves, covetous, boasters, proud, blasphemers, disobedient to parents, unthankful, unholy,
>
> Without natural affection, trucebreakers, false accusers, incontinent, fierce, despisers of those that are good,
>
> Traitors, heady, highminded, lovers of pleasures more than lovers of God;
>
> Having a form of godliness, but denying the power thereof: from such turn away.

Part 3

Praise

PSALMS 115:18

But we will bless the Lord from this time forth and for evermore. Praise the Lord.

PSALMS 107:31

Oh that men would praise the Lord for his goodness, and for his wonderful works to the children of men!

PSALMS 135:3

Praise the Lord; for the Lord is good: sing praises unto his name; for it is pleasant.

PSALMS 68:4

Sing unto God, sing praises to his name: extol him that rideth upon the heavens by his name Jah, and rejoice before him.

PSALMS 66:1-2

Make a joyful noise unto God, all ye lands:

Sing forth the honor of his name: make his praise glorious.

PSALMS 48:1

Great is the Lord, and greatly to be praised in the city of our God, in the mountain of his holiness.

139

Knowing His Promises

PSALMS 150:1-6

Praise ye the Lord. Praise God in his sanctuary: praise him in the firmament of his power.

Praise him for his mighty acts: praise him according to his excellent greatness.

Praise him with the sound of the trumpet: praise him with the psaltery and harp.

Praise him with the timbrel and dance: praise him with stringed instruments and organs.

Praise him upon the loud cymbals: praise him upon the high sounding cymbals.

Let every thing that hath breath praise the Lord. Praise ye the Lord.

PSALMS 117:1

O praise the Lord, all ye nations: praise him, all ye people.

PSALMS 111:1

Praise ye the Lord. I will praise the Lord with my whole heart, in the assembly of the upright, and in the congregation.

PSALMS 149:1

Praise ye the Lord. Sing unto the Lord a new song, and his praise in the congregation of saints.

PSALMS 135:1

Praise ye the Lord. Praise ye the name of the Lord; praise him, O ye servants of the Lord.

Part 3 • **Renew My Spirit** • *Praise*

Bless the Lord, O my soul: and all that is within me, bless his holy name.

Bless the Lord, O my soul, and forget not all his benefits:

Who forgiveth all thine iniquities; who healeth all thy diseases;

Who redeemeth thy life from destruction; who crowneth thee with loving kindness and tender mercies;

Who satisfieth thy mouth with good things; so that thy youth is renewed like the eagle's.

The Lord executeth righteousness and judgment for all that are oppressed.

He made known his ways unto Moses, his acts unto the children of Israel.

The Lord is merciful and gracious, slow to anger, and plenteous in mercy.

He will not always chide: neither will he keep his anger for ever.

He hath not dealt with us after our sins; nor rewarded us according to our iniquities.

For as the heaven is high above the earth, so great is his mercy toward them that fear him.

As far as the east is from the west, so far hath he removed our transgressions from us.

Like as a father pitieth his children, so the Lord pitieth them that fear him.

Knowing His Promises

JEREMIAH 20:13

Sing unto the Lord, praise ye the Lord: for he hath delivered the soul of the poor from the hand of evildoers.

PSALMS 117:1-2

O praise the Lord, all ye nations: praise him, all ye people.

For his merciful kindness is great toward us: and the truth of the Lord endureth for ever. Praise ye the Lord.

PSALMS 109:30

I will greatly praise the Lord with my mouth; yea, I will praise him among the multitude.

PSALMS 40:3

And he hath put a new song in my mouth, even praise unto our God: many shall see it, and fear, and shall trust in the Lord.

PSALMS 113:1

Praise ye the Lord. Praise, O ye servants of the Lord, praise the name of the Lord.

PSALMS 35:28

And my tongue shall speak of thy righteousness and of thy praise all the day long.

PSALMS 145:10

All thy works shall praise thee, O Lord; and thy saints shall bless thee.

PSALMS 51:15

O Lord, open thou my lips; and my mouth shall shew forth thy praise.

PSALMS 30:12

> To the end that my glory may sing praise to thee, and not be silent. O Lord my God, I will give thanks unto thee for ever.

PSALMS 107:1-2

> O give thanks unto the Lord, for he is good: for his mercy endureth for ever.

> Let the redeemed of the Lord say so, whom he hath redeemed from the hand of the enemy;

PSALMS 34:1

> I will bless the Lord at all times: his praise shall continually be in my mouth.

HEBREWS 13:15

> By him therefore let us offer the sacrifice of praise to God continually, that is, the fruit of our lips giving thanks to his name.

PSALMS 69:30

> I will praise the name of God with a song, and will magnify him with thanksgiving.

DEUTERONOMY 10:21

> He is thy praise, and he is thy God, that hath done for thee these great and terrible things, which thine eyes have seen.

PSALMS 86:12

> I will praise thee, O Lord my God, with all my heart: and I will glorify thy name for evermore.

143

Knowing His Promises

PSALMS 65:1

Praise waiteth for thee, O God, in Sion: and unto thee shall the vow be performed.

PSALMS 118:21

I will praise thee: for thou hast heard me, and art become my salvation.

PSALMS 139:14

I will praise thee; for I am fearfully and wonderfully made: marvellous are thy works; and that my soul knoweth right well.

1 CHRONICLES 29:13

Now therefore, our God, we thank thee, and praise thy glorious name.

PSALMS 57:9

I will praise thee, O Lord, among the people: I will sing unto thee among the nations.

PSALMS 104:33

I will sing unto the Lord as long as I live: I will sing praise to my God while I have my being.

PSALMS 56:4

In God I will praise his word, in God I have put my trust; I will not fear what flesh can do unto me.

PSALMS 33:2

Praise the Lord with harp: sing unto him with the psaltery and an instrument of ten strings.

PART 3 • RENEW MY SPIRIT

Trust

MARK 5:35-36

While he yet spake, there came from the ruler of the synagogue's house certain which said, Thy daughter is dead: why troublest thou the Master any further?

As soon as Jesus heard the word that was spoken, he saith unto the ruler of the synagogue, Be not afraid, only believe.

1 PETER 5:6-7

Humble yourselves therefore under the mighty hand of God, that he may exalt you in due time:

Casting all your care upon him; for he careth for you.

MARK 4:19

And the cares of this world, and the deceitfulness of riches, and the lusts of other things entering in, choke the word, and it becometh unfruitful.

PSALMS 78:21-22

Therefore the Lord heard this, and was wroth: so a fire was kindled against Jacob, and anger also came up against Israel;

Because they believed not in God, and trusted not in his salvation:

ROMANS 10:17

So then faith cometh by hearing, and hearing by the word of God.

145

Knowing His Promises

LUKE 10:41-42

And Jesus answered and said unto her, Martha, Martha, thou art careful and troubled about many things: But one thing is needful: and Mary hath chosen that good part, which shall not be taken away from her.

MATTHEW 8:26

And he saith unto them, Why are ye fearful, O ye of little faith? Then he arose, and rebuked the winds and the sea; and there was a great calm.

PHILIPPIANS 4:6-7

Be careful for nothing; but in every thing by prayer and supplication with thanksgiving let your requests be made known unto God.

And the peace of God, which passeth all understanding, shall keep your hearts and minds through Christ Jesus.

MATTHEW 6:25

Therefore I say unto you, Take no thought for your life, what ye shall eat, or what ye shall drink; nor yet for your body, what ye shall put on. Is not the life more than meat, and the body than raiment?

JOHN 8:36

If the Son therefore shall make you free, ye shall be free indeed.

PSALMS 42:5-6

Why art thou cast down, O my soul? and why art thou disquieted in me? hope thou in God: for I shall yet praise him for the help of his countenance.

O my God, my soul is cast down within me: therefore will I remember thee from the land of Jordan, and of the Hermonites, from the hill Mizar.

Part 3 • **Renew My Spirit** • *Trust*

PSALMS 18:4-17

The sorrows of death compassed me, and the floods of ungodly men made me afraid.

The sorrows of hell compassed me about: the snares of death prevented me.

In my distress I called upon the Lord, and cried unto my God: he heard my voice out of his temple, and my cry came before him, even into his ears.

Then the earth shook and trembled; the foundations also of the hills moved and were shaken, because he was wroth.

There went up a smoke out of his nostrils, and fire out of his mouth devoured: coals were kindled by it.

He bowed the heavens also, and came down: and darkness was under his feet.

And he rode upon a cherub, and did fly: yea, he did fly upon the wings of the wind.

He made darkness his secret place; his pavilion round about him were dark waters and thick clouds of the skies.

At the brightness that was before him his thick clouds passed, hail stones and coals of fire.

The Lord also thundered in the heavens, and the Highest gave his voice; hail stones and coals of fire.

Yea, he sent out his arrows, and scattered them; and he shot out lightnings, and discomfited them.

Then the channels of waters were seen, and the foundations of the world were discovered at thy rebuke, O Lord, at the blast of the breath of thy nostrils.

147

TRUST

Knowing His Promises

He sent from above, he took me, he drew me out of many waters.

He delivered me from my strong enemy, and from them which hated me: for they were too strong for me.

COLOSSIANS 1:9-13

For this cause we also, since the day we heard it, do not cease to pray for you, and to desire that ye might be filled with the knowledge of his will in all wisdom and spiritual understanding;

That ye might walk worthy of the Lord unto all pleasing, being fruitful in every good work, and increasing in the knowledge of God;

Strengthened with all might, according to his glorious power, unto all patience and long suffering with joyfulness;

Giving thanks unto the Father, which hath made us meet to be partakers of the inheritance of the saints in light:

Who hath delivered us from the power of darkness, and hath translated us into the kingdom of his dear Son:

PSALMS 31:23-24

O love the Lord, all ye his saints: for the Lord preserveth the faithful, and plentifully rewardeth the proud doer.

Be of good courage, and he shall strengthen your heart, all ye that hope in the Lord.

ISAIAH 59:1

Behold, the Lord's hand is not shortened, that it cannot save; neither his ear heavy, that it cannot hear:

Part 3 • **Renew My Spirit** • *Trust*

JOHN 14:1

Let not your heart be troubled: ye believe in God, believe also in me.

EPHESIANS 1:15-19

Wherefore I also, after I heard of your faith in the Lord Jesus, and love unto all the saints,

Cease not to give thanks for you, making mention of you in my prayers;

That the God of our Lord Jesus Christ, the Father of glory, may give unto you the spirit of wisdom and revelation in the knowledge of him:

The eyes of your understanding being enlightened; that ye may know what is the hope of his calling, and what the riches of the glory of his inheritance in the saints,

And what is the exceeding greatness of his power to usward who believe, according to the working of his mighty power,

1 CORINTHIANS 7:32-35

But I would have you without carefulness. He that is unmarried careth for the things that belong to the Lord, how he may please the Lord:

But he that is married careth for the things that are of the world, how he may please his wife.

There is difference also between a wife and a virgin. The unmarried woman careth for the things of the Lord, that she may be holy both in body and in spirit: but she that is married careth for the things of the world, how she may please her husband.

And this I speak for your own profit; not that I may cast a snare upon you, but for that which is comely, and that ye may attend upon the Lord without distraction.

149

Knowing His Promises

HEBREWS 11:1-2,6

Now faith is the substance of things hoped for, the evidence of things not seen.

For by it the elders obtained a good report.

But without faith it is impossible to please him: for he that cometh to God must believe that he is, and that he is a rewarder of them that diligently seek him.

ISAIAH 61:1-3

The Spirit of the Lord God is upon me; because the Lord hath anointed me to preach good tidings unto the meek; he hath sent me to bind up the brokenhearted, to proclaim liberty to the captives, and the opening of the prison to them that are bound;

To proclaim the acceptable year of the Lord, and the day of vengeance of our God; to comfort all that mourn;

To appoint unto them that mourn in Zion, to give unto them beauty for ashes, the oil of joy for mourning, the garment of praise for the spirit of heaviness; that they might be called trees of righteousness, the planting of the Lord, that he might be glorified.

LUKE 21:34

And take heed to yourselves, lest at any time your hearts be overcharged with surfeiting, and drunkenness, and cares of this life, and so that day come upon you unawares.

JOHN 8:32

And ye shall know the truth, and the truth shall make you free.

PSALMS 31:22

> For I said in my haste, I am cut off from before thine eyes: nevertheless thou heardest the voice of my supplications when I cried unto thee.

MATTHEW 13:58

> And he did not many mighty works there because of their unbelief.

MATTHEW 6:28

> And why take ye thought for raiment? Consider the lilies of the field, how they grow; they toil not, neither do they spin:

JOSHUA 4:24

> That all the people of the earth might know the hand of the Lord, that it is mighty: that ye might fear the Lord your God for ever.

ISAIAH 53:1

> Who hath believed our report? and to whom is the arm of the Lord revealed?

HEBREWS 13:5

> Let your conversation be without covetousness; and be content with such things as ye have: for he hath said, I will never leave thee, nor forsake thee.

NUMBERS 11:23

> And the Lord said unto Moses, Is the Lord's hand waxed short? thou shalt see now whether my word shall come to pass unto thee or not.

TRUST

Knowing His Promises

MATTHEW 6:33-34

But seek ye first the kingdom of God, and his righteousness; and all these things shall be added unto you.

Take therefore no thought for the morrow: for the morrow shall take thought for the things of itself. Sufficient unto the day is the evil thereof.

MARK 4:40

And he said unto them, Why are ye so fearful? how is it that ye have no faith?

MATTHEW 6:31-32

Therefore take no thought, saying, What shall we eat? or, What shall we drink? or, Wherewithal shall we be clothed?

(For after all these things do the Gentiles seek:) for your heavenly Father knoweth that ye have need of all these things.

PSALMS 37:7-8

Rest in the Lord, and wait patiently for him: fret not thyself because of him who prospereth in his way, because of the man who bringeth wicked devices to pass.

Cease from anger, and forsake wrath: fret not thyself in any wise to do evil.

PSALMS 127:1-2

Except the Lord build the house, they labor in vain that build it: except the Lord keep the city, the watchman waketh but in vain.

It is vain for you to rise up early, to sit up late, to eat the bread of sorrows: for so he giveth his beloved sleep.

JEREMIAH 17:7-10

Blessed is the man that trusteth in the Lord, and whose hope the Lord is.

For he shall be as a tree planted by the waters, and that spreadeth out her roots by the river, and shall not see when heat cometh, but her leaf shall be green; and shall not be careful in the year of drought, neither shall cease from yielding fruit.

The heart is deceitful above all things, and desperately wicked: who can know it?

I the Lord search the heart, I try the reins, even to give every man according to his ways, and according to the fruit of his doings.

HEBREWS 12:2

Looking unto Jesus the author and finisher of our faith; who for the joy that was set before him endured the cross, despising the shame, and is set down at the right hand of the throne of God.

LUKE 12:26-27

If ye then be not able to do that thing which is least, why take ye thought for the rest?

Consider the lilies how they grow: they toil not, they spin not; and yet I say unto you, that Solomon in all his glory was not arrayed like one of these.

LUKE 21:14-15

Settle it therefore in your hearts, not to meditate before what ye shall answer:

For I will give you a mouth and wisdom, which all your adversaries shall not be able to gainsay nor resist.

Knowing His Promises

MATTHEW 10:19-20

But when they deliver you up, take no thought how or what ye shall speak: for it shall be given you in that same hour what ye shall speak.

For it is not ye that speak, but the Spirit of your Father which speaketh in you.

PSALMS 37:40

And the Lord shall help them, and deliver them: he shall deliver them from the wicked, and save them, because they trust in him.

PSALMS 131:1-3

Lord, my heart is not haughty, nor mine eyes lofty: neither do I exercise myself in great matters, or in things too high for me.

Surely I have behaved and quieted myself, as a child that is weaned of his mother: my soul is even as a weaned child.

Let Israel hope in the Lord from henceforth and for ever.

MATTHEW 14:29-31

And he said, Come. And when Peter was come down out of the ship, he walked on the water, to go to Jesus.

But when he saw the wind boisterous, he was afraid; and beginning to sink, he cried, saying, Lord, save me.

And immediately Jesus stretched forth his hand, and caught him, and said unto him, O thou of little faith, wherefore didst thou doubt?

PSALMS 37:5

Commit thy way unto the Lord; trust also in him; and he shall bring it to pass.

PROVERBS 16:3

Commit thy works unto the Lord, and thy thoughts shall be established.

LUKE 12:22-24

And he said unto his disciples, Therefore I say unto you, Take no thought for your life, what ye shall eat; neither for the body, what ye shall put on.

The life is more than meat, and the body is more than raiment.

Consider the ravens: for they neither sow nor reap; which neither have storehouse nor barn; and God feedeth them: how much more are ye better than the fowls?

LUKE 9:62

And Jesus said unto him, No man, having put his hand to the plough, and looking back, is fit for the kingdom of God.

PSALMS 55:22

Cast thy burden upon the Lord, and he shall sustain thee: he shall never suffer the righteous to be moved.

JAMES 1:6-8

But let him ask in faith, nothing wavering. For he that wavereth is like a wave of the sea driven with the wind and tossed.

For let not that man think that he shall receive any thing of the Lord.

A double minded man is unstable in all his ways.

Knowing His Promises

And when they bring you unto the synagogues, and unto magistrates, and powers, take ye no thought how or what thing ye shall answer, or what ye shall say:

Part 3

PART 3 • RENEW MY SPIRIT

Love of God

MATTHEW 22:37-39

Jesus said unto him, Thou shalt love the Lord thy God with all thy heart, and with all thy soul, and with all thy mind.

This is the first and great commandment.

And the second is like unto it, Thou shalt love thy neighbor as thyself.

PSALMS 103:13

Like as a father pitieth his children, so the Lord pitieth them that fear him.

DEUTERONOMY 30:20

That thou mayest love the Lord thy God, and that thou mayest obey his voice, and that thou mayest cleave unto him: for he is thy life, and the length of thy days: that thou mayest dwell in the land which the Lord sware unto thy fathers, to Abraham, to Isaac, and to Jacob, to give them.

EPHESIANS 2:4-5

But God, who is rich in mercy, for his great love wherewith he loved us,

Even when we were dead in sins, hath quickened us together with Christ, (by grace ye are saved;)

Knowing His Promises

1 John 3:1

Behold, what manner of love the Father hath bestowed upon us, that we should be called the sons of God: therefore the world knoweth us not, because it knew him not.

Psalms 47:4

He shall choose our inheritance for us, the excellency of Jacob whom he loved. Selah.

Proverbs 15:9

The way of the wicked is an abomination unto the Lord: but he loveth him that followeth after righteousness.

Psalms 89:33

Nevertheless my loving kindness will I not utterly take from him, nor suffer my faithfulness to fail.

Psalms 37:4

Delight thyself also in the Lord: and he shall give thee the desires of thine heart.

Romans 5:5

And hope maketh not ashamed; because the love of God is shed abroad in our hearts by the Holy Ghost which is given unto us.

Mark 12:32-33

And the scribe said unto him, Well, Master, thou hast said the truth: for there is one God; and there is none other but he:

And to love him with all the heart, and with all the understanding, and with all the soul, and with all the strength, and to love his neighbor as himself, is more than all whole burnt offerings and sacrifices.

1 JOHN 4:15-21

Whosoever shall confess that Jesus is the Son of God,
God dwelleth in him, and he in God.

And we have known and believed the love that God hath
to us. God is love; and he that dwelleth in love dwelleth
in God, and God in him.

Herein is our love made perfect, that we may have boldness in the day of judgment: because as he is, so are we
in this world.

There is no fear in love; but perfect love casteth out fear:
because fear hath torment. He that feareth is not made
perfect in love.

We love him, because he first loved us.

If a man say, I love God, and hateth his brother, he is a
liar: for he that loveth not his brother whom he hath
seen, how can he love God whom he hath not seen?

And this commandment have we from him, That he who
loveth God love his brother also.

2 JOHN 1:6

And this is love, that we walk after his commandments.
This is the commandment, That, as ye have heard from
the beginning, ye should walk in it.

1 JOHN 4:12

No man hath seen God at any time. If we love one
another, God dwelleth in us, and his love is perfected in
us.

ROMANS 5:8

But God commendeth his love toward us, in that while
we were yet sinners, Christ died for us.

159

Knowing His Promises

DEUTERONOMY 7:9

Know therefore that the Lord thy God, he is God, the faithful God, which keepeth covenant and mercy with them that love him and keep his commandments to a thousand generations;

1 JOHN 4:19-20

We love him, because he first loved us.

If a man say, I love God, and hateth his brother, he is a liar: for he that loveth not his brother whom he hath seen, how can he love God whom he hath not seen?

JOHN 3:16-17

For God so loved the world, that he gave his only begotten Son, that whosoever believeth in him should not perish, but have everlasting life.

For God sent not his Son into the world to condemn the world; but that the world through him might be saved.

2 CORINTHIANS 9:7

Every man according as he purposeth in his heart, so let him give; not grudgingly, or of necessity: for God loveth a cheerful giver.

1 JOHN 2:5

But whoso keepeth his word, in him verily is the love of God perfected: hereby know we that we are in him.

ISAIAH 43:4

Since thou wast precious in my sight, thou hast been honorable, and I have loved thee: therefore will I give men for thee, and people for thy life.

PSALMS 91:14

Because he hath set his love upon me, therefore will I deliver him: I will set him on high, because he hath known my name.

PSALMS 63:5-6

My soul shall be satisfied as with marrow and fatness; and my mouth shall praise thee with joyful lips:

When I remember thee upon my bed, and meditate on thee in the night watches.

1 CORINTHIANS 13:4-8

Charity suffereth long, and is kind; charity envieth not; charity vaunteth not itself, is not puffed up,

Doth not behave itself unseemly, seeketh not her own, is not easily provoked, thinketh no evil;

Rejoiceth not in iniquity, but rejoiceth in the truth;

Beareth all things, believeth all things, hopeth all things, endureth all things.

Charity never faileth: but whether there be prophecies, they shall fail; whether there be tongues, they shall cease; whether there be knowledge, it shall vanish away.

PHILIPPIANS 1:9

And this I pray, that your love may abound yet more and more in knowledge and in all judgment;

JOHN 14:21

He that hath my commandments, and keepeth them, he it is that loveth me: and he that loveth me shall be loved of my Father, and I will love him, and will manifest myself to him.

161

Knowing His Promises

1 JOHN 2:15

Love not the world, neither the things that are in the world. If any man love the world, the love of the Father is not in him.

PSALMS 31:23-24

O love the Lord, all ye his saints: for the Lord preserveth the faithful, and plentifully rewardeth the proud doer.

Be of good courage, and he shall strengthen your heart, all ye that hope in the Lord.

PSALMS 146:8

The Lord openeth the eyes of the blind: the Lord raiseth them that are bowed down: the Lord loveth the righteous:

PSALMS 97:10

Ye that love the Lord, hate evil: he preserveth the souls of his saints; he delivereth them out of the hand of the wicked.

DEUTERONOMY 11:1

Therefore thou shalt love the Lord thy God, and keep his charge, and his statutes, and his judgments, and his commandments, always.

JOHN 5:42

But I know you, that ye have not the love of God in you.

PSALMS 18:1

I will love thee, O Lord, my strength.

PSALMS 145:20

The Lord preserveth all them that love him: but all the wicked will he destroy.

ISAIAH 56:6-7

Also the sons of the stranger, that join themselves to the Lord, to serve him, and to love the name of the Lord, to be his servants, every one that keepeth the sabbath from polluting it, and taketh hold of my covenant;

Even them will I bring to my holy mountain, and make them joyful in my house of prayer: their burnt offerings and their sacrifices shall be accepted upon mine altar; for mine house shall be called an house of prayer for all people.

MARK 12:29-30

And Jesus answered him, The first of all the commandments is, Hear, O Israel; The Lord our God is one Lord:

And thou shalt love the Lord thy God with all thy heart, and with all thy soul, and with all thy mind, and with all thy strength: this is the first commandment.

DEUTERONOMY 6:5

And thou shalt love the Lord thy God with all thine heart, and with all thy soul, and with all thy might.

DEUTERONOMY 30:16

In that I command thee this day to love the Lord thy God, to walk in his ways, and to keep his commandments and his statutes and his judgments, that thou mayest live and multiply: and the Lord thy God shall bless thee in the land whither thou goest to possess it.

1 JOHN 4:12-13

Beloved, think it not strange concerning the fiery trial which is to try you, as though some strange thing happened unto you:

But rejoice, inasmuch as ye are partakers of Christ's sufferings; that, when his glory shall be revealed, ye may be glad also with exceeding joy.

163

Knowing His Promises

JOHN 14:23

Jesus answered and said unto him, If a man love me, he will keep my words: and my Father will love him, and we will come unto him, and make our abode with him.

2 THESSALONIANS 2:16-17

Now our Lord Jesus Christ himself, and God, even our Father, which hath loved us, and hath given us everlasting consolation and good hope through grace,

Comfort your hearts, and stablish you in every good word and work.

Part 3

Prayer

PSALMS 5:3

My voice shalt thou hear in the morning, O Lord; in the morning will I direct my prayer unto thee, and will look up.

PSALMS 88:13

But unto thee have I cried, O Lord; and in the morning shall my prayer prevent thee.

PSALMS 143:8

Cause me to hear thy loving kindness in the morning; for in thee do I trust: cause me to know the way wherein I should walk; for I lift up my soul unto thee.

PSALMS 55:16-17

As for me, I will call upon God; and the Lord shall save me.

Evening, and morning, and at noon, will I pray, and cry aloud: and he shall hear my voice.

LUKE 6:12

And it came to pass in those days, that he went out into a mountain to pray, and continued all night in prayer to God.

1 THESSALONIANS 5:17

Pray without ceasing.

165

PRAYER

Knowing His Promises

HEBREWS 4:16

Let us therefore come boldly unto the throne of grace, that we may obtain mercy, and find grace to help in time of need.

MATTHEW 6:5-7,9-13

And when thou prayest, thou shalt not be as the hypocrites are: for they love to pray standing in the synagogues and in the corners of the streets, that they may be seen of men. Verily I say unto you, They have their reward.

But thou, when thou prayest, enter into thy closet, and when thou hast shut thy door, pray to thy Father which is in secret; and thy Father which seeth in secret shall reward thee openly.

But when ye pray, use not vain repetitions, as the heathen do: for they think that they shall be heard for their much speaking.

After this manner therefore pray ye: Our Father which art in heaven, Hallowed be thy name.

Thy kingdom come, Thy will be done in earth, as it is in heaven.

Give us this day our daily bread.

And forgive us our debts, as we forgive our debtors.

And lead us not into temptation, but deliver us from evil: For thine is the kingdom, and the power, and the glory, for ever. Amen.

PSALMS 5:1

Give ear to my words, O Lord, consider my meditation.

Part 3 • **Renew My Spirit** • *Prayer*

PSALMS 40:1

> I waited patiently for the Lord; and he inclined unto me, and heard my cry.

MATTHEW 18:19-20

> Again I say unto you, That if two of you shall agree on earth as touching any thing that they shall ask, it shall be done for them of my Father which is in heaven.
>
> For where two or three are gathered together in my name, there am I in the midst of them.

ACTS 16:25-26

> And at midnight Paul and Silas prayed, and sang praises unto God: and the prisoners heard them.
>
> And suddenly there was a great earthquake, so that the foundations of the prison were shaken: and immediately all the doors were opened, and every one's bands were loosed.

MATTHEW 7:7-8

> Ask, and it shall be given you; seek, and ye shall find; knock, and it shall be opened unto you:
>
> For every one that asketh receiveth; and he that seeketh findeth; and to him that knocketh it shall be opened.

MATTHEW 21:22

> And all things, whatsoever ye shall ask in prayer, believing, ye shall receive.

MARK 11:24

> Therefore I say unto you, What things soever ye desire, when ye pray, believe that ye receive them, and ye shall have them.

167

PRAYER

Knowing His Promises

PHILIPPIANS 4:6-7

Be careful for nothing; but in every thing by prayer and supplication with thanksgiving let your requests be made known unto God.

And the peace of God, which passeth all understanding, shall keep your hearts and minds through Christ Jesus.

1 TIMOTHY 2:8

I will therefore that men pray every where, lifting up holy hands, without wrath and doubting.

EPHESIANS 6:16,18

Above all, taking the shield of faith, wherewith ye shall be able to quench all the fiery darts of the wicked.

Praying always with all prayer and supplication in the Spirit, and watching thereunto with all perseverance and supplication for all saints;

1 TIMOTHY 2:1

I exhort therefore, that, first of all, supplications, prayers, intercessions, and giving of thanks, be made for all men;

LUKE 2:37

And she was a widow of about fourscore and four years, which departed not from the temple, but served God with fastings and prayers night and day.

ACTS 6:4

But we will give ourselves continually to prayer, and to the ministry of the word.

ACTS 13:3

And when they had fasted and prayed, and laid their hands on them, they sent them away.

Part 3 • **Renew My Spirit** • *Prayer*

JAMES 5:14,16-18

Is any sick among you? let him call for the elders of the church; and let them pray over him, anointing him with oil in the name of the Lord:

Confess your faults one to another, and pray one for another, that ye may be healed. The effectual fervent prayer of a righteous man availeth much.

Elias was a man subject to like passions as we are, and he prayed earnestly that it might not rain: and it rained not on the earth by the space of three years and six months.
And he prayed again, and the heaven gave rain, and the earth brought forth her fruit.

PSALMS 42:8

Yet the Lord will command his loving kindness in the day time, and in the night his song shall be with me, and my prayer unto the God of my life.

PSALMS 109:4

For my love they are my adversaries: but I give myself unto prayer.

ACTS 14:23

And when they had ordained them elders in every church, and had prayed with fasting, they commended them to the Lord, on whom they believed.

MATTHEW 17:21

Howbeit this kind goeth not out but by prayer and fasting.

PRAYER

Prayer

Knowing His Promises

1 Corinthians 7:5

Defraud ye not one the other, except it be with consent for a time, that ye may give yourselves to fasting and prayer; and come together again, that Satan tempt you not for your incontinency.

Deuteronomy 4:29-31

But if from thence thou shalt seek the Lord thy God, thou shalt find him, if thou seek him with all thy heart and with all thy soul.

When thou art in tribulation, and all these things are come upon thee, even in the latter days, if thou turn to the Lord thy God, and shalt be obedient unto his voice;

(For the Lord thy God is a merciful God;) he will not forsake thee, neither destroy thee, nor forget the covenant of thy fathers which he sware unto them.

2 Chronicles 7:13-15

If I shut up heaven that there be no rain, or if I command the locusts to devour the land, or if I send pestilence among my people;

If my people, which are called by my name, shall humble themselves, and pray, and seek my face, and turn from their wicked ways; then will I hear from heaven, and will forgive their sin, and will heal their land.

Now mine eyes shall be open, and mine ears attent unto the prayer that is made in this place.

Job 33:26

He shall pray unto God, and he will be favorable unto him: and he shall see his face with joy: for he will render unto man his righteousness.

PSALMS 9:10

> And they that know thy name will put their trust in thee: for thou, Lord, hast not forsaken them that seek thee.

PSALMS 18:3

> I will call upon the Lord, who is worthy to be praised: so shall I be saved from mine enemies.

PSALMS 32:6

> For this shall every one that is godly pray unto thee in a time when thou mayest be found: surely in the floods of great waters they shall not come nigh unto him.

PSALMS 34:15,17

> The eyes of the Lord are upon the righteous, and his ears are open unto their cry.

> The righteous cry, and the Lord heareth, and delivereth them out of all their troubles.

PSALMS 37:4-5

> Delight thyself also in the Lord: and he shall give thee the desires of thine heart.

> Commit thy way unto the Lord; trust also in him; and he shall bring it to pass.

PSALMS 38:15

> For in thee, O Lord, do I hope: thou wilt hear, O Lord my God.

PSALMS 69:33

> For the Lord heareth the poor, and despiseth not his prisoners.

Knowing His Promises

PSALMS 86:7

In the day of my trouble I will call upon thee: for thou wilt answer me.

PSALMS 91:15

He shall call upon me, and I will answer him: I will be with him in trouble; I will deliver him, and honor him.

PSALMS 145:18

The Lord is nigh unto all them that call upon him, to all that call upon him in truth.

PROVERBS 3:5-6

Trust in the Lord with all thine heart; and lean not unto thine own understanding.

In all thy ways acknowledge him, and he shall direct thy paths.

PROVERBS 15:8,29

The sacrifice of the wicked is an abomination to the Lord: but the prayer of the upright is his delight.

The Lord is far from the wicked: but he heareth the prayer of the righteous.

ISAIAH 19:20

And it shall be for a sign and for a witness unto the Lord of hosts in the land of Egypt: for they shall cry unto the Lord because of the oppressors, and he shall send them a savior, and a great one, and he shall deliver them.

ISAIAH 55:6

Seek ye the Lord while he may be found, call ye upon him while he is near:

ISAIAH 58:9

Then shalt thou call, and the Lord shall answer; thou shalt cry, and he shall say, Here I am. If thou take away from the midst of thee the yoke, the putting forth of the finger, and speaking vanity;

ISAIAH 65:24

And it shall come to pass, that before they call, I will answer; and while they are yet speaking, I will hear.

JEREMIAH 29:12-13

Then shall ye call upon me, and ye shall go and pray unto me, and I will hearken unto you.

And ye shall seek me, and find me, when ye shall search for me with all your heart.

JEREMIAH 33:3

Call unto me, and I will answer thee, and shew thee great and mighty things, which thou knowest not.

LAMENTATIONS 3:25

The Lord is good unto them that wait for him, to the soul that seeketh him.

ROMANS 8:26

Likewise the Spirit also helpeth our infirmities: for we know not what we should pray for as we ought: but the Spirit itself maketh intercession for us with groanings which cannot be uttered.

I JOHN 3:22

And whatsoever we ask, we receive of him, because we keep his commandments, and do those things that are pleasing in his sight.

Knowing His Promises

JOHN 14:14

If ye shall ask any thing in my name, I will do it.

PSALMS 56:9

When I cry unto thee, then shall mine enemies turn back: this I know; for God is for me.

JAMES 1:5

If any of you lack wisdom, let him ask of God, that giveth to all men liberally, and upbraideth not; and it shall be given him.

PSALMS 10:17

Lord, thou hast heard the desire of the humble: thou wilt prepare their heart, thou wilt cause thine ear to hear:

1 KINGS 17:22

And the Lord heard the voice of Elijah; and the soul of the child came into him again, and he revived.

PSALMS 65:2

O thou that hearest prayer, unto thee shall all flesh come.

1 CHRONICLES 4:10

And Jabez called on the God of Israel, saying, Oh that thou wouldest bless me indeed, and enlarge my coast, and that thine hand might be with me, and that thou wouldest keep me from evil, that it may not grieve me! And God granted him that which he requested.

JOHN 9:31

Now we know that God heareth not sinners: but if any man be a worshipper of God, and doeth his will, him he heareth.

JOHN 15:7

If ye abide in me, and my words abide in you, ye shall ask what ye will, and it shall be done unto you.

PSALMS 118:5

I called upon the Lord in distress: the Lord answered me, and set me in a large place.

PROVERBS 10:24

The fear of the wicked, it shall come upon him: but the desire of the righteous shall be granted.

PSALMS 118:6

The Lord is on my side; I will not fear: what can man do unto me?

HEBREWS 11:6

But without faith it is impossible to please him: for he that cometh to God must believe that he is, and that he is a rewarder of them that diligently seek him.

JOHN 15:16

Ye have not chosen me, but I have chosen you, and ordained you, that ye should go and bring forth fruit, and that your fruit should remain: that whatsoever ye shall ask of the Father in my name, he may give it you.

HEBREWS 10:23

Let us hold fast the profession of our faith without wavering; (for he is faithful that promised;)

2 KINGS 20:11

And Isaiah the prophet cried unto the Lord: and he brought the shadow ten degrees backward, by which it had gone down in the dial of Ahaz.

Knowing His Promises

1 JOHN 5:14-15

And this is the confidence that we have in him, that, if we ask any thing according to his will, he heareth us:

And if we know that he hear us, whatsoever we ask, we know that we have the petitions that we desired of him.

PSALMS 50:15

And call upon me in the day of trouble: I will deliver thee, and thou shalt glorify me.

PSALMS 138:3

In the day when I cried thou answeredst me, and strengthenedst me with strength in my soul.

PSALMS 65:5

By terrible things in righteousness wilt thou answer us, O God of our salvation; who art the confidence of all the ends of the earth, and of them that are afar off upon the sea:

DEUTERONOMY 4:7

For what nation is there so great, who hath God so nigh unto them, as the Lord our God is in all things that we call upon him for?

EPHESIANS 3:20

Now unto him that is able to do exceeding abundantly above all that we ask or think, according to the power that worketh in us,

EXODUS 33:17

And the Lord said unto Moses, I will do this thing also that thou hast spoken: for thou hast found grace in my sight, and I know thee by name.

AMOS 5:4

For thus saith the Lord unto the house of Israel, Seek ye me, and ye shall live:

LUKE 21:36

Watch ye therefore, and pray always, that ye may be accounted worthy to escape all these things that shall come to pass, and to stand before the Son of man.

JOHN 15:16

Ye have not chosen me, but I have chosen you, and ordained you, that ye should go and bring forth fruit, and that your fruit should remain: that whatsoever ye shall ask of the Father in my name, he may give it you.

JOHN 16:23-24

And in that day ye shall ask me nothing. Verily, verily, I say unto you, Whatsoever ye shall ask the Father in my name, he will give it you.

Hitherto have ye asked nothing in my name: ask, and ye shall receive, that your joy may be full.

JAMES 4:8

Draw nigh to God, and he will draw nigh to you. Cleanse your hands, ye sinners; and purify your hearts, ye double minded.

LUKE 18:1

And he spake a parable unto them to this end, that men ought always to pray, and not to faint;

PSALMS 2:12

Kiss the Son, lest he be angry, and ye perish from the way, when his wrath is kindled but a little. Blessed are all they that put their trust in him.

PRAYER

Knowing His Promises

MARK 9:23

Jesus said unto him, If thou canst believe, all things are possible to him that believeth.

ROMANS 10:12,17

For there is no difference between the Jew and the Greek: for the same Lord over all is rich unto all that call upon him.

So then faith cometh by hearing, and hearing by the word of God.

HEBREWS 13:6

So that we may boldly say, The Lord is my helper, and I will not fear what man shall do unto me.

Prayer Journal

Notes

Answers to the back cover questions

Where can you find these verses answers?

Question 1, Answer Hebrews 11:1
Question 2, Answer Phil. 1:6
Question 3, Proverbs 9:9
Question 4, Isaiah 1:19

Quote the following verses answers

Psalms 18:2
"The Lord is my rock, and my fortress, and my deliverer; my God, my strength, in whom I will trust my buckler, and the horn of my salvation, and my high tower."

Romans 12:1
"I beseech you therfore brethren, by the mercies of God, that ye present your bodies a living sacrifice, holy, acceptable unto God, which is your reasonable service."

Matthew 6:33
"But seek ye first the kingdom of God, and his righteousness; and all these things shall be added unto you."

John 10:10
"The theif cometh not, but for to steal, and to kill and destroy: I am come that they might have life and that they might have it more abundantly."